Read Write Inc.

Literacy and Language Handbook

Janey Pursglove and Charlotte Raby
Series developed by Ruth Miskin

OXFORD
UNIVERSITY PRESS

OXFORD
UNIVERSITY PRESS

Great Clarendon Street, Oxford, OX2 6DP,
United Kingdom

Oxford University Press is a department of the University of Oxford.
It furthers the University's objective of excellence in research, scholarship, and education
by publishing worldwide. Oxford is a registered trade mark
of Oxford University Press in the UK and in certain other countries

First Edition published in 2013

British Library Cataloguing in Publication Data
Data available

ISBN: 978-0-19-849372-3

7 9 10 8 6

Paper used in the production of this book is a natural, recyclable product made from wood grown in sustainable forests. The manufacturing process conforms to the environmental regulations of the country of origin.

Printed in Great Britain by Ashford Colour Press

Acknowledgements

The publishers would like to thank Jenny Roberts for her
contribution to the grammar activities.

Cover: Alexandra Huard

Illustrations by: Anthony Browne; Maria Cirstina; Ross Collins; Mark Draisey; Lizzie Finlay; Andrew Painter; Garry Parsons; Korky Paul; Dusan Pavlic; Mike Phillips; Tony Ross; Victor Tavares

Design by Q2A

Contents

Introduction

What is Literacy and Language?

Literacy and Language is a complete literacy programme for children in Years 2–6 (Primary 3–7). It is designed to stimulate and challenge children's thinking and create enthusiastic, lifelong readers and writers.

It provides explicit guidance for developing children's reading comprehension and writing composition with support for teaching grammar, vocabulary development, critical thinking and spoken language. It gives you all the support you need to teach outstanding, consistent literacy lessons every day, and to deliver the new National Curriculum confidently.

The core purpose of the programme is to ensure that children, as the National Curriculum aims state:

- read easily, fluently and with good understanding
- develop the habit of reading widely and often for both pleasure and information
- acquire a wide vocabulary
- use grammar correctly
- appreciate our rich and varied literary heritage
- write clearly, accurately and coherently, adapting their language and style in and for a range of contexts, purposes and audiences
- use discussion in order to learn; they should be able to elaborate and explain clearly their understanding and ideas
- are competent in the arts of speaking and listening, making formal presentations, demonstrating to others and participating in debate

Literacy and Language resources for each year:

an **Anthology** of complete stories, plays, poems and non-fiction texts	a **Pupils' Book** containing writing, grammar, comprehension and vocabulary activities related to the Anthology texts	a **Homework Book** providing further practice and consolidation of grammar points and writing tasks	**Software** with a wide variety of teacher-led activities and teacher support, for use on an interactive whiteboard	a **Handbook** giving clear day-by-day lesson plans for each Unit

Resources

Anthology

Literacy and Language is based on Anthologies of carefully chosen complete stories, plays, poems and non-fiction texts by leading children's authors including Michael Morpurgo, Jeremy Strong, Roger McGough, Geraldine McCaughrean, Jamila Gavin, Ted Hughes and Kaye Umansky.

The range of stories, plays, poems and non-fiction texts in *Literacy and Language* provide an opportunity for children to study texts which are absorbing, challenging and deep enough to dive into, while being accessible to all children.

The children's increasing familiarity with a wide range of stories, plays, poems and non-fiction texts will generate a desire for more reading for pleasure. Wider reading lists are provided for every Unit.

All the texts in the Anthology are complete and are just the right length for children to read during the lesson and to develop reading stamina.

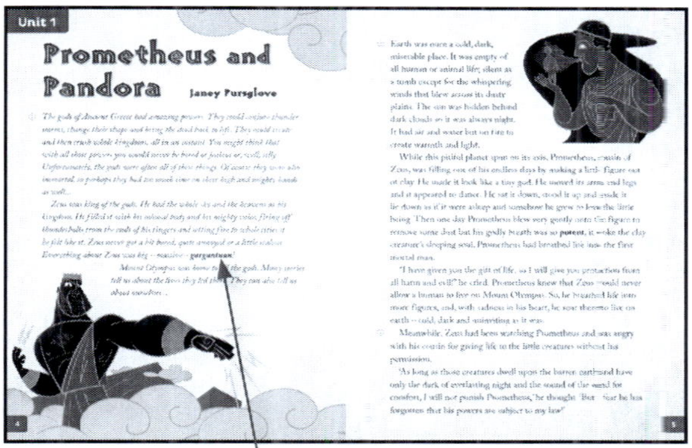

All the fiction and non-fiction texts include rarer vocabulary, which the children explore through Word power activities prior to reading the text.

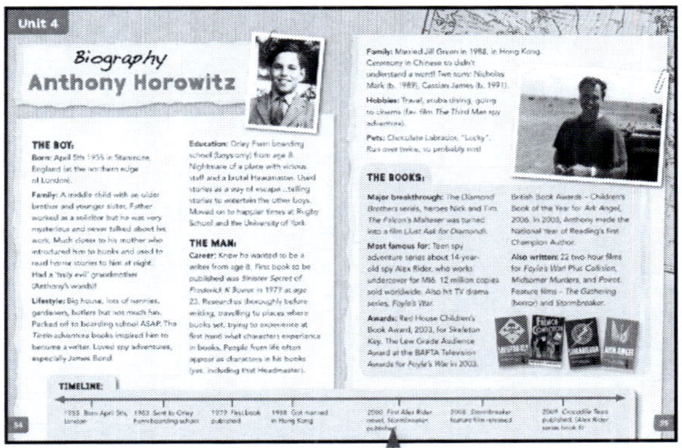

Each non-fiction text is a model of a particular form with a clear purpose, aimed at a specific audience. The high-interest, often humorous non-fiction texts provide further stimulus for reading widely and often.

Pupils' Book

Lively activities in the Pupils' Book develop children's writing, grammar, comprehension and vocabulary skills. The activities are linked to the Anthology texts and help children consolidate and apply what they are learning.

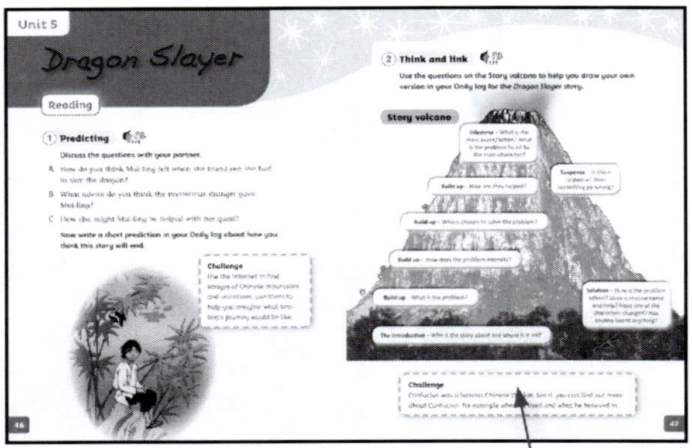

Grammar is taught in context and through writing to make it meaningful for children.

'**Challenge**' activities are included as extension activiti to encourage children to work independently ar to extend their wider knowledg

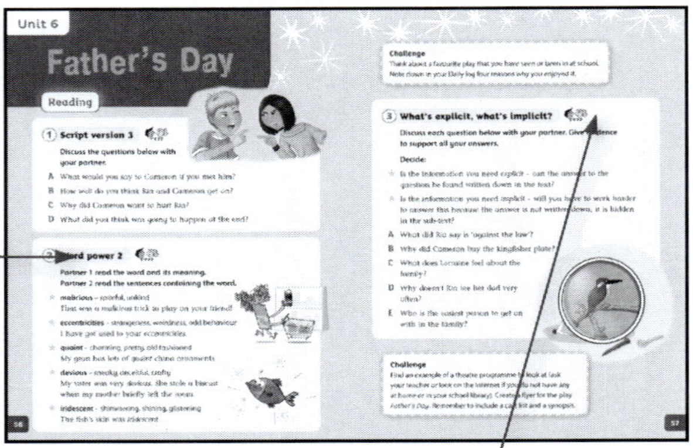

Each Unit has **activities on 'Power words'** – ambitious words to enhance children's spoken vocabulary and ultimately their vocabulary for writing.

Partner work is embedded in the programme – many of the activities are rooted in discussion, which helps to develop children's spoken English.

Homework Book

The Homework Book contains weekly activities which allow children to practise and embed the grammar, writing and other language and literacy skills they have learnt in the lessons.

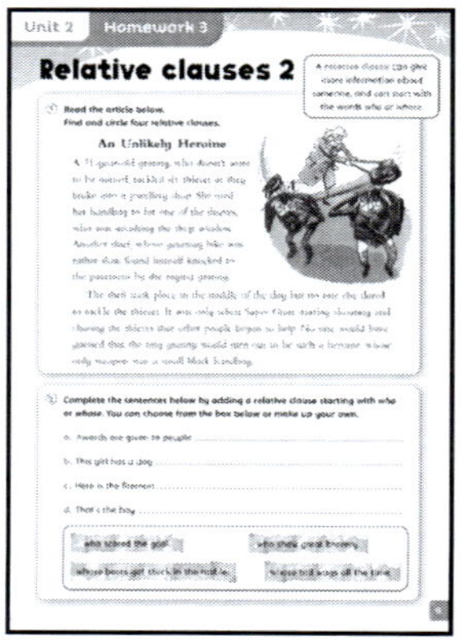

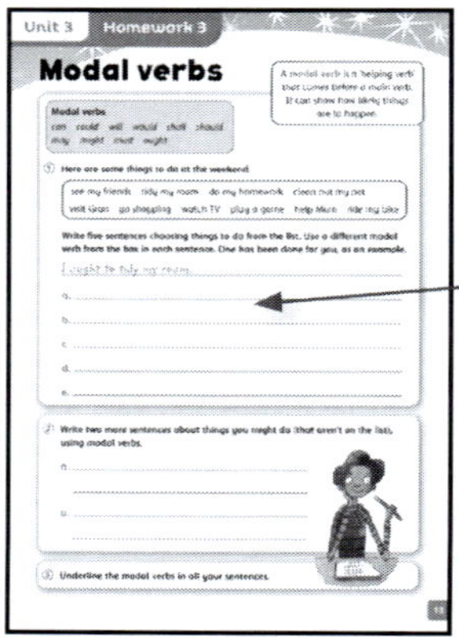

The activities are accessible and engaging, with age-appropriate glossaries and information boxes to ensure children can work independently at home.

Software

The Software is integral to the programme and is used for whole class teaching. It contains a range of resources to support your teaching.

There are fully illustrated texts, including stories, plays, poems and non-fiction texts from the Anthology, to display and explore as a class.

Audio and video clips are used to introduce drama activities or stimulate discussion.

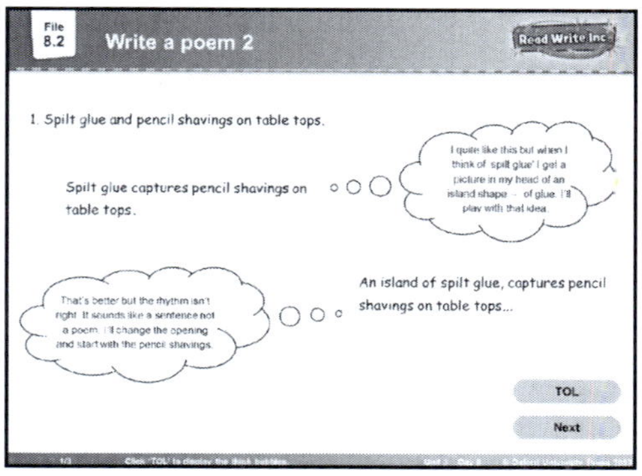

There are **modelled writing scripts** for the teacher to show how a text is built up, including how to 'Think out loud' to show children how to develop ideas.

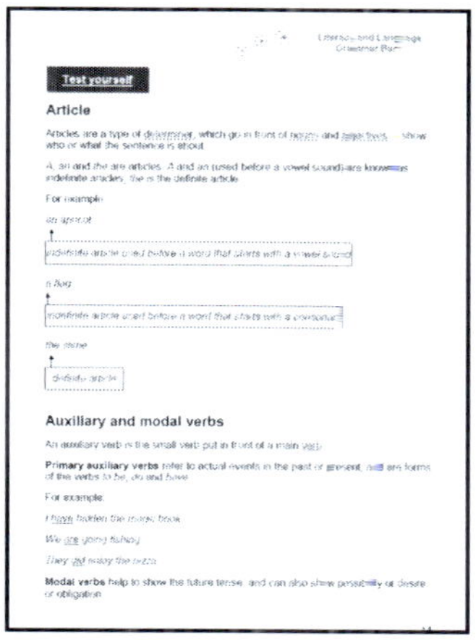

A **Grammar Bank** gives teachers clear explanations about every aspect of grammar in the new National Curriculum and practice tests for children (see p.9).

Files include:

- video, audio performances of the poems and plays, radio interviews, music and images
- drag and drop language activities
- writing plans which can be printed out for class use
- 'Think out loud' teacher scripts for modelled writing
- 'Power words' for classroom display
- ready-prepared 'Write a story' texts for modelled writing
- editable timetables.

The Software booklet provides more detailed information about the features of the Software.

All this support makes it possible for you to teach an outstanding literacy lesson every day.

Teaching Handbook

Teachers are given comprehensive, structured support from the detailed day-by-day lesson plans in the Teaching Handbook and timetables.

Overview timetables are provided in the Teaching Handbook and as editable files on the Software.

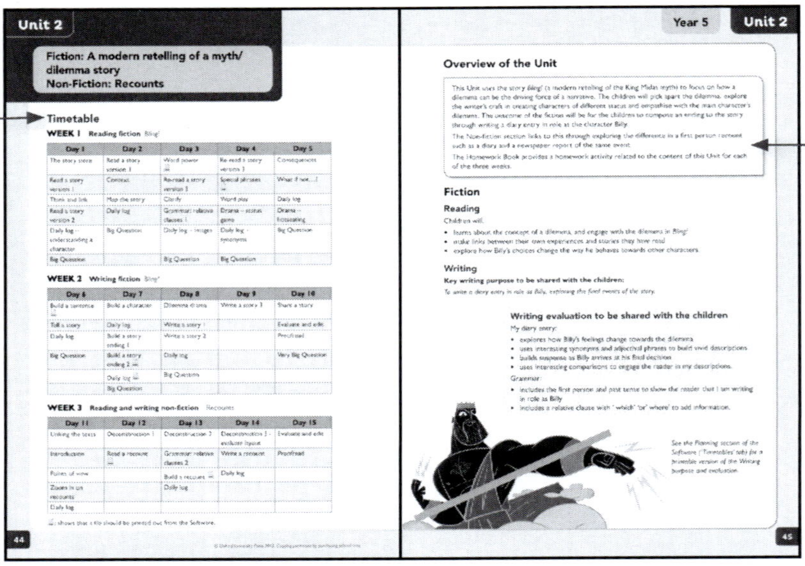

An overview of each Unit includes assessment criteria for reading and writing.

Lesson plans give detailed guidance for each activity.

Activities are clearly matched to the new National Curriculum.

Partner work ensures that every child is speaking every day, enriching their spoken English.

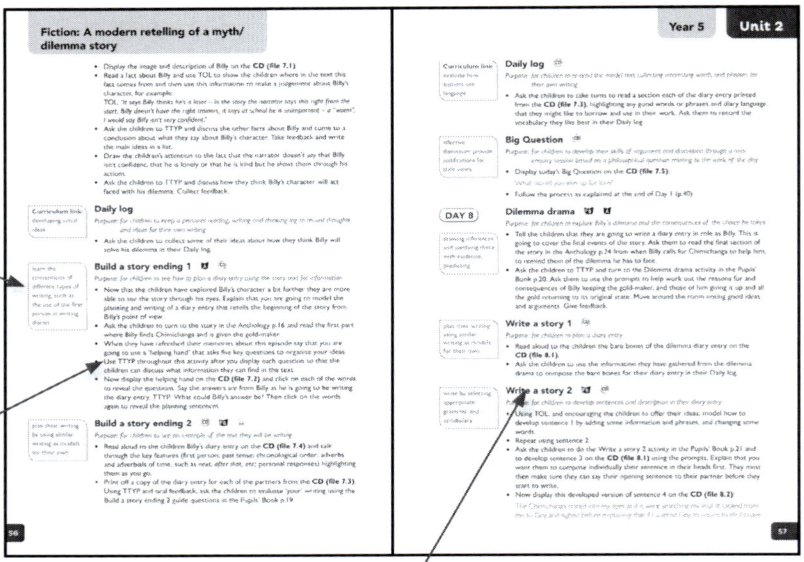

Children write every day, building up ideas, planning, developing longer pieces of writing, then evaluating, editing and proofreading their work.

What will children be taught?

Comprehension skills

At the heart of *Literacy and Language* is the enjoyment of and engagement with a variety of texts. Children are encouraged to take their own meaning from each text, becoming independent and critical thinkers. Comprehension activities are designed to help children to infer, summarise, question, clarify, predict and argue a point of view. The children also make connections between texts and their own experiences. The programme approach integrates reading, writing, thinking, and spoken language in all activities, to ensure the daily development of children's comprehension and wider literacy skills.

Grammar

Children are taught the importance of using grammar correctly, so they can communicate clearly and convey their meaning effectively. Comprehensive guidance is provided for teachers, supported by engaging Software, Pupils' Book and Homework Book activities.

Children meet examples of the grammar point they will study in the context of the story, playscript, poem or non-fiction text in the Anthology. The teacher then explains the grammar concept to the children, often using the Software and an activity in the Pupils' Book. Children are also taught the grammatical terms. When the teacher models the writing process the grammar concept is included so that children can see how to use it in their writing. When children do their main writing task they are reminded to include the grammar point as it is listed in the evaluation criteria. Children consolidate their knowledge of the grammar concept through activities in the Homework Book.

Grammar Bank

A Grammar Bank on the Software provides teachers with explanations about every aspect of grammar in the new National Curriculum. It contains a detailed, cross-referenced glossary of grammar terminology with clear examples and 'test yourself' exercises for teachers, with answers included. There are also grammar tests for children that provide practice in the type of questions they will meet in the English Grammar, Punctuation and Spelling Test.

The Grammar Bank allows teachers to consolidate their grammar skills and includes 'test yourself' sections.

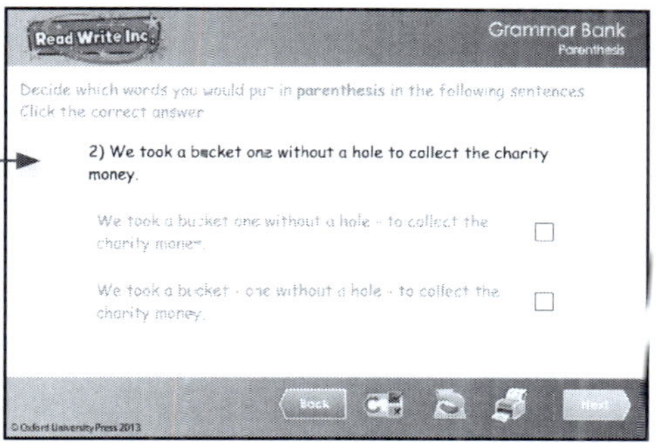

Three grammar, punctuation and vocabulary tests for each year provide meaningful practice for children for the English Grammar, Punctuation and Spelling Test.

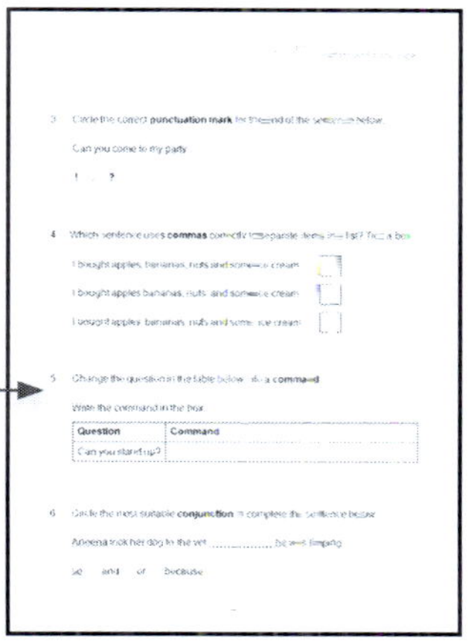

Writing

Daily writing is at the heart of *Literacy and Language*. Alongside the main, extended writing activities, opportunities are taken every day to create shorter pieces of writing. This allows children to focus on very specific skills, build up their confidence and stamina for writing, and develop their understanding of audience and purpose.

As the new National Curriculum recommends, children are shown the process of writing. Using the resources for modelled writing and 'Thinking out loud', you can show what is involved in being a writer: making choices, alterations and additions while monitoring for sense and meaning. This de-mystifies the writing process for children while demonstrating the 'magic' of creating different effects with language. Writing in action shows children the power of language.

What they read, talk about and see through teacher modelling encourages children to experiment with language to express their thoughts and ideas accurately and independently. Most importantly, daily writing opportunities help children to develop a belief in themselves as writers.

Vocabulary development

The greater the children's vocabulary and the complexity of the language they hear and read, the richer their writing will be. The stories, plays, poems and non-fiction texts in the programme all include ambitious vocabulary. Before children read the texts, they are taught the meanings of more challenging words – both in the context of the story and in real life situations. The teacher and children use the vocabulary throughout the lesson, but also through the week, until the words become familiar. These new words and phrases are displayed and collected from one week to the next, keeping the favourite and most useful words displayed throughout the programme.

Spoken language

The new National Curriculum places huge emphasis upon spoken language. It states, 'The quality of and variety of language that pupils hear and speak are vital for developing their vocabulary, grammar and their understanding for reading and writing.'

Teaching children to articulate their thoughts and ideas out loud and to communicate what they know and understand is critical to the success of *Literacy and Language*. Children are taught to orally rehearse what they will write before putting pen to paper.

Teachers 'Think out loud' to show children what is involved in becoming an effective reader and writer. You can show children how you clarify and modify your understanding of what you read – how you infer and predict; build pictures in your mind; identify what's important; summarise key points; and importantly, persevere when things get tricky. In the same way, children are expected to 'Think out loud' with a partner to check their own understanding so their thinking is made clear to themselves as well as to you.

Literacy and Language uses carefully constructed partner work to make this possible. *Read Write Inc.* partner work is pacey, structured and meaningful – it keeps the children engaged throughout the lesson. Children answer every question with a partner, comment on each other's ideas, clarify each other's thinking, and build upon each other's thoughts and ideas. The teacher listens in carefully, selects children to give feedback and then selects others to build upon what they say. The teacher asks questions to take their thinking further and clears up any misconceptions.

Spelling

Read Write Inc. Spelling covers the National Curriculum spelling requirements and can be used alongside *Literacy and Language*.

How does the programme work?

Literacy and Language comprises six Units of work per year group. The Units are designed to be used over three weeks, but can also be used more flexibly, e.g. over a longer period if necessary as there is ample material and stimulus in the programme to extend tasks.

Whilst all literacy skills are developed throughout the programme, each week has a *particular* focus:

- Week 1 Reading fiction
- Week 2 Writing fiction
- Week 3 Reading and writing non-fiction

Children write every day in their Daily log (notebook) so that writing becomes a habit. They record their thoughts, ideas, and reactions to the text, often as mind maps and story maps – some of which they will draw on for extended writing activities in Weeks 2 and 3.

Grammar activities are woven into the programme on the Software and in the Pupils' Book. In addition, the Homework Book provides an opportunity for children to consolidate and practise their grammar, writing and other literacy skills at home.

Thinking and discussion skills are practised through a daily 'Big Question' which is a philosophical question that children debate so that their spoken language is developed every day.

Week 1: Reading fiction

The story store

The main story (or poem or playscript) the children study in each Unit is introduced via a brief discussion of other texts containing similar themes, some of which will be familiar to most children. Summaries of these texts are provided in the Story store on the Software. This activity helps children to make connections between texts and their own experiences.

Read a story versions 1, 2 and 3

Literacy and Language uses a three layers of text approach to teaching reading and writing. Children are introduced to the text via Story version 1, 2 and 3.

Story version 1 introduces the children to the characters, setting, and plot through about ten sentences – the 'bare bones' of the story. This allows all children to access the basic story straight away. The ending is never revealed at this stage to ensure the children are motivated to want to read the full story.

Story version 2 is a little longer than Story version 1. It gives the children more information about the characters, setting and plot. This shows children how language can be used to change or develop readers' understanding of texts.

Reading Story version 1 and Story version 2 first means that when the full story is revealed in Story version 3, which is in the Anthology, the children can focus all their attention on the subtleties, nuances and their own interpretations of the text. The staged and guided access into the story means that children who need more support are undaunted by a challenging text and can immerse themselves in the world of the story as successfully as the children who need least support.

Week 2: Writing fiction

Build a story 1, 2 and 3

Having explored a text through three layers of meaning, from its simplest level to its most complex, children then see a new text being composed through the planning, oral rehearsing, drafting and editing stages. The teacher shows how a story is 'built up' via three layers of development (Build a story 1, 2 and 3). Using the pre-prepared resources, you are fully supported in the role of a writer as you model the composition of a text. This modelled writing deepens children's understanding of the writing process and enables them to compose confidently themselves.

Write a story 1, 2 and 3

With your support, the children then mirror the process you have modelled, drafting and revising so that they write ambitiously and accurately as they compose their own extended piece of writing.

The Software provides two versions of a story being written – Write a story 1 and Write a story 2. Through drama activities, teacher modelling and partner work, children build on these story frameworks, adding their own ideas, developing sentences and using them as models for planning their own plots, structures and characters. These prepare children to write the full story – Write a story 3.

Week 3: Reading and writing non-fiction

The fiction and non-fiction texts in each Unit are linked via one of the 'Big Questions' that children debated in the Fiction weeks. Children explore examples of the non-fiction text type, focusing on audience, purpose, form and style through Deconstruction 1, 2 and 3 activities which are designed to reveal the conventions of specific text types. Then they use what they have learnt to plan and draft their own pieces of writing, with an audience in mind, through Write a… 1 and 2 (discussion text/explanation text/instruction text, etc. depending on the text type). A final piece is then written (Write a… 3) presented and evaluated through self and peer assessment.

Core activities

The core activities encourage children to engage fully with the text as they explore character, motivation, settings and themes.

Word power

Powerful, evocative vocabulary is explained and explored before children encounter it in the story, play, poem or non-fiction text. Teachers and children are also encouraged to use the 'Power words' outside the context of the story to ensure they become part of the children's own vocabulary store.

Think and link

Used at different points in the programme, this ensures that children question what they are reading and connect it to their wider reading, own experiences and current understanding of the world.

What if not…?

An opportunity for children to speculate on how a story would change if the writer altered any one aspect of character, plot or setting, developing their awareness of how one is affected by the other, e.g. in *This is NOT a Fairy Tale*, we ask What if not *wise*? What if Luke had been *stupid* like the rest of the villagers?

Build a sentence

Build a sentence is used to build a vivid, engaging description. The starting point is often a single word or a short phrase which is chosen because it is particularly powerful or unusual. The activity is used, with My turn/Your turn, to build up a sentence from a simple fragment to an ambitious, complex sentence that provides children with a model of good writing in microcosm. Teachers model making choices out loud, making changes and improvements, and repeating their sentence to themselves to ensure they can remember it. Sentences can be built up out loud, or written down.

Jump in

The purpose of Jump in is to help children remember vocabulary and phrases from the story. Jump in is used in *Literacy and Language* on subsequent readings of the fiction texts, to help children remember and assimilate the 'Power words' and 'Special phrases'. Once they get to know the story, ask them to join in the reading of the words in bold. Exaggerate particular words and phrases and use actions and facial expressions to help.

Daily logs

Children write in a Daily log (notebook) to:

- record responses to what they have read, thought and talked about
- experiment with vocabulary and text structures
- make notes, mind and story maps, diagrams and plans
- collect and paste related artefacts – tickets, photos, leaflets and drawings from home.

Big Question

A 'Big Question' is asked at the end of Days 1–8 and discussion should take about 10 minutes. These questions explore an idea linked to an aspect of the text covered that day, e.g. after reading a re-telling of the King Midas myth (Bling) the children debate: What would you give up to have your greatest wish? The aim of the Big Question is to develop spoken language and argument skills. Children learn to justify ideas with reasons, negotiate, evaluate and build on the ideas of others, select the appropriate register for effective communication, as well as think in a deeper way about the more abstract issues that come from the text. Children are encouraged to express their opinions and enjoy a context in which there may be no right or wrong answers, just their own carefully considered opinions.

On Day 10 children vote on which Big Question to revisit and explore more fully as a 'Very Big Question' (see p.36). This provides an opportunity for children to develop or revise their opinions. See the Very Big Question organisation below on p.17.

On Day 11 the non-fiction text is introduced through a brief re-examination of one of the Big Questions already discussed in the fiction weeks, helping children to make links between their own ideas and contextualising the new non-fiction text. For example, in Unit 3, children study poems about cities and one of the Big Questions is: Should natural environments be destroyed to make way for humans? This is briefly revisited on Day 11 when introducing persuasive writing which features non-fiction texts about parkland being destroyed to make way for a football stadium.

Picture Books in Year 2

The same concepts and structures are used in *Literacy and Language* across Years 2–6. In Year 2, however, the Story store is enhanced by the use of high quality picture books as an introduction to the themes to be explored in the Anthology story, play or poem.

Authors and illustrators include Tony Ross, Anthony Browne, Jeanne Willis and Korky Paul.

Differentiation – guided assistance

It has been assumed that children in the *Literacy and Language* groups will all be fluent readers but not necessarily working at the same comprehension level. Differentiation is achieved by the amount of support pupils need in order to learn something new. The guidance in *Literacy and Language* ensures that children who need least support receive the necessary challenge and that others receive the necessary assistance to understand the texts they read and to write confidently.

The range of teaching and learning strategies embedded within the *Literacy and Language* resources allow you to ensure that all children develop their ability to understand the texts they read, use the spoken word confidently and become accomplished writers.

Teachers support and challenge the children by:

- developing comprehension using the three layers of text approach for reading, allowing access to engaging and challenging texts for all children
- modelling your thought processes in planning for writing and editing using 'Think out loud' and the three layers of text approach for writing
- preparing children for writing using oral rehearsal
- providing differentiated writing frames where necessary
- asking and encouraging children to ask questions, with an emphasis on allowing thinking and talking time
- using partner and small group work developed to a high level to provide peer support and challenge
- encouraging use of the Daily logs to enrich and extend children's thinking, providing a 'safe' place for recording thoughts and ideas and to experiment with short pieces of writing
- using Challenge activities in Years 5 and 6 for class extension work.

Assessment and marking

Assessment is integral to the whole *Literacy and Language* programme. Partner discussion helps teachers assess what and how children are learning throughout the lesson.

The specific focus for both reading and writing is set out at the beginning of each Unit, along with the key purpose and evaluation criteria for children's main writing composition. Each set of partners is provided with a copy of the writing Evaluation criteria (see the Planning section of the Software, and navigate to the 'Timetables' tab for these) at the start of the writing process and this is used as a guide for editing and evaluating their own and their partner's work. The criteria are included in the Pupils' Book for selected Units, and as PowerPoints on the Software, to show that they are integral to the writing process. They also form the basis for the teacher's marking. Teachers are encouraged to mark the children's work thoroughly and give advice on their next steps based upon the Evaluation criteria.

Commenting on Daily logs

Teachers explain that the Daily log is an important part of being a writer – it is to a writer what a sketch book is to an artist. The children know that the logs will not be 'marked' in the same way as their exercise books. Teachers read the children's notes and ideas and respond with thoughtful notes and suggestions. These should be written in pencil, not pen; it will be like a dialogue on paper. Children should be aware that their privacy will be respected and that ideas from their Daily log will not be shared with others without their permission. Although the Daily log is for notes and ideas, it should be stressed that this book is special – it is not a rough book or jotter. Children can leave the front page empty so that, at the end of the year, they can make a contents page for the year's work.

How do you get started?

Book training

Ruth Miskin Training provides a one- or two-day in-school training course or a one-day central training course. A knowledgeable and experienced trainer ensures you can teach the new National Curriculum confidently, using *Literacy and Language*. Please note: *Literacy and Language* should be taught by qualified teachers.

Appoint the *Literacy and Language* leader. Choose a confident and organised teacher to meet the other teachers every week for 20 minutes to discuss one particular aspect of *Literacy and Language*, demonstrate lessons to teachers, observe other teachers, evaluate children's progress and teachers' marking.

Training can be booked at: www.ruthmiskintraining.com

How does the programme fit with Read Write Inc. Phonics?

As soon as children have completed *Read Write Inc. Phonics*, or are reading at NC Level 2a, they are ready to start *Literacy and Language*. Children who finish *Read Write Inc. Phonics* during Year 2 join a Year 2 *Literacy and Language* class. Children who finish in Year 3 join a Year 3 *Literacy and Language* class, and so on. We develop the same teaching strategies and principles used in *Read Write Inc. Phonics*:

Full participation: this is fundamental to *Literacy and Language*. Teachers use 'Think out loud' to show the children how to analyse, plan and organise their ideas. 'My turn/Your turn' is also used to practise key activities and, crucially, partner work ensures that all children participate in the whole lesson.

Positive teaching: children learn at a much faster pace in an assertive and positive climate. They talk more readily in an atmosphere free from anger and tension. Praise for effective partner work is crucial.

Pace: each Unit has been planned to take three weeks. However, teachers might choose to add in extra time for some activities. You may also want to plan time for children to present and publish some of their final compositions.

Purpose: every part of the lesson has a very clear purpose. Please read the explanation behind the core activities on p.12. It is important to make the purpose of each activity transparent and easy to understand using child-friendly language.

Passion: this is a very supportive and detailed programme, which is why it works so well. However, it is the energy, enthusiasm and passion that teachers put into the lessons that bring the teaching and learning to life. Passionate teaching has impact.

Setting up Literacy and Language in your classroom

Timetable 70 minutes for *Literacy and Language* lessons. We also recommend that schools plan for an additional 20 minutes for Storytime every day. Suggested stories and poems to read to children are listed on www.ruthmiskintraining.com. In the Overview chart on pp.18–19, there are also suggestions for stories and books for wider reading which will link to the themes and genres explored in the Units.

Management signals

Use these signals to ensure teaching is effective and consistent throughout the school.

The 'stop' signal: when all children are engaged in partner work, you need to be able to get their attention quickly and easily without raising your voice. Hold your hand in the air and do not talk whilst it is raised. When children see the signal they should finish what they are saying and raise one hand in response. Do not start talking until everyone has returned the signal and you have lowered your hand.

'My turn/Your turn' signal (MT/YT): there are times when you will need children to copy what you do. *My turn:* touch your chest with your palm when it's your turn. *Your turn:* open your palm to children when it's their turn.

The 'Turn to your partner' signal (TTYP): before you ask a question, tap two fingers together to warn children they will need to turn to their partners to answer. Explain that the 'hands up' system for answering questions will not be used. Ask children to put one hand on their head if they need clarification or have a question to ask.

The 'Perfect partner position': partners should sit side-by-side and shoulder-to-shoulder. (If they face each other the noise level increases.) Number the partners 1 and 2. Children keep the same number for the duration of the whole Unit. See the Planning section of the Software and navigate to the 'Extras' tab for further guidance on choosing partners, and activities to ensure partners work effectively together.

Planning and preparation

All the planning is ready for you to use. However, a thorough understanding of the programme's multi-layered and integrated approach to teaching fiction, non-fiction and grammar is vital. The more prepared you are, the more successful your children will be.

First, gain a thorough overview of the whole Unit. Read the story and non-fiction texts in the Anthology, followed by the teachers' notes in the Handbook, and the activities in the Pupils' Book and Software. You will see how the individual layers unfold; how the reading activities feed into the writing and how the 'Big Questions' weave together the fiction and non-fiction texts. Each activity builds upon the next.

Study the timetable at the beginning of each Unit – it provides an overview of the activities for each day and shows when you need to print out any files from the Software such as evaluation sheets, modelled writing prompts, words for display, etc.

Prepare for your lessons using the teaching notes for the Unit. You could also use and adapt the flexible planning sheets on the Software.

Organising discussion

Setting ground rules for discussion

The ground rules for discussion should inform the whole school policy on teaching and learning so they become fundamental to every lesson in every curriculum area. Children should be taught, explicitly, the rules for working in a group or with a partner and take part in regular evaluations of what makes for effective discussion – see the Planning section of the Software, and navigate to the 'Extras' tab for the Effective discussion poster. Although the rules are similar for all ages, children's responses increase in complexity and sophistication year-by-year.

Display the Effective discussion poster in a prominent position. Praise the children for specific behaviour when partners co-operate successfully.

Short answers
Explain to the children that you will sometimes require a one- or two-word answer to questions – use a finger and thumb to show 'small'. This action tells partners to turn back to you quickly once they have said their answer to their partner.

One, two, three: if there is only one answer to the question, say '*One, two, three,*' and ask children to call out the answer together.

Popcorn: if there are lots of different one-word answers use Popcorn – children call out their answers in the pauses between other answers.

Wave: sweep your arm across the room in a wave. Children call out their answer as your arm sweeps over them.

Longer answers to explain why
Ask a question, then ask partners to TTYP (Turn to your partner). Listen in to different partnerships each time, sometimes building on their ideas. Do not get too involved with one partnership as it is important to observe how well all sets of partners work together – particularly in the early days. Do not give children too long to answer or let the discussion tail off. Importantly, make sure children carry on talking until you raise your hand to stop. It is very disruptive to discussion when children raise their hands/show thumbs or use any other signal to show that they have an answer ready. Select partnerships with helpful contributions to feed back to the group or do this on their behalf.

In-depth answers to consider different viewpoints, challenge claims politely, negotiate an agreement
As above but go backwards and forwards, asking other partnerships to build on the contributions of others.

Very Big Question organisation

For the extended 'Very Big Question' discussion, make sure the children are seated so that they can all see each other. Set aside 20–30 minutes to allow a full discussion. Act as the facilitator and avoid taking over or dominating the discussion. Ensure that all children are allowed to express their points of view and make every attempt to elicit responses from other children to what has been said rather than simply accepting a series of opinions with no real acknowledgement of others' ideas and opinions.

You can vary the way you organise the children, e.g. have a whole group discussion, smaller groups or pairs who discuss and then come together as one large group. Avoid 'jigsawing' as you want the children to develop their ability to sustain and deepen discussions beyond their first responses.

The Big Questions and the Very Big Questions are not just about developing language and social skills. They are vital opportunities for children to explore ways of thinking about and perceiving the world, themselves and others and of universal themes and ideas stimulated by their reading.

Overview chart

Unit	Unit 1	Unit 2	Unit 3
Main grammar focus for the Unit	Devices to build cohesion within a paragraph Linking ideas across paragraphs	Relative clauses	Modal verbs Adverbs of possibility
Fiction text/s	*Prometheus and Pandora* by Janey Pursglove (A myth)	*Bling!* by Jon Blake (A modern re-telling of a myth/dilemma story)	'Goodnight Stroud' by Pie Corbett 'Last Night, I Saw The City Breathing' by Andrew Fusek Peters (Poetic style)
Fiction focus	Children analyse the importance of different characters to the development of the story and examine the role of the narrator as storyteller. Differences between oral and written storytelling are explored and used to support the children's own writing and storytelling.	The story is a modern re-telling of the King Midas myth and the Unit focuses on how a dilemma can be a driving force of a narrative. The children create characters of different status and empathise with the main character's dilemma. They compose an ending to the story through a diary entry written in role as the main character.	Children study two poems about cities which have been chosen for their similar theme, strong imagery, rich vocabulary and use of powerful personification. They compose a free verse poem.
Suggestions for wider reading	*Percy Jackson and The Lightning Thief* – Rick Riordan *Heroes of Olympus* – Rick Riordan *Persephone* – Sally Pomme Clayton *Pandora* – Robert Burleigh *Pandora's Box* – Rose Impey	*Artemis Fowl* – Eoin Colfer *Coraline* – Neil Gaiman *Diamond of Drury Lane* – Julia Golding *Lionboy* – Zizou Corder *The Midas Touch* – Jan Mark Juan Wijngaard *The Chocolate Touch* – Patrick Skene Catling	Any other books by Jeremy Strong *Ratburger, Gangsta Granny, The Boy in the Dress, Billionaire Boy, Mr Stink* – David Walliams *The Diary of a Wimpy Kid* – Jeff Kinney *Mr Gum* books – Andy Stanton *Alex Rider* books – Anthony Horowitz *The Power of Five* books – Anthony Horowitz
Non-fiction texts/s	'How to Write Instructions' 'How to Write a Greek Myth' 'Have a go at... Chocolate Chip Ice Cream' (Instructions)	'Bravery Award for Fire Hero Boy' 'Newshound' 'Beach Bonanza!' (Recounts)	'Meet the Monster!' 'Meet the Future!' (Persuasive writing)
Non-fiction focus	The non-fiction part of the Unit develops children's understanding of the features of instructional writing. They will analyse, evaluate and write instructions. The outcome is for children to write instructions for making sherbet, which are followed and evaluated by their peers.	The non-fiction links to the fiction through exploring the difference between a first person recount, such as a diary, and a newspaper report of the same event. Children compose their own newspaper report based on a real-life rescue and adapt it for the radio.	The non-fiction explores persuasive writing and is linked to the 'cities' theme of the poetry. The children write a persuasive presentation which they present to the class in the role of residents at a public meeting to discuss plans for building a football stadium.

	Unit 4	Unit 5	Unit 6
	Brackets, dashes or commas to indicate parenthesis	Converting nouns or adjectives into verbs using suffixes Verb prefixes	Use of commas to clarify meaning or avoid ambiguity
	This Is NOT a Fairy Tale by Jeremy Strong (A story by a significant children's author)	*Dragon Slayer* by Gill Howell (A story from another culture)	*Father's Day* by Lou Kuenzler (A playscript, dramatic conventions)
	This Unit explores the work of the author Jeremy Strong. Focusing on one of his short stories and other examples of his work the children find out about his style and explore how he creates his stories as a series of humorous episodes with pace and excitement. They use various techniques to help them understand how to create characters and dialogue. They write their own episode that continues the short story.	This Unit explores story structure using a story from another culture. *Dragon Slayer* is an adventure story set in China and provides an exciting model for children to explore using pace and suspense to add excitement to their narratives.	Children study a playscript, *Father's Day*, about step-sibling rivalry. The author uses a range of dramatic conventions to explore subtleties of character and the conflicting emotions experienced within families. Children study the plot and sub-plot and dramatic convention. Elements of performance are also included. Children look at the stages of development of a script, then go on to write an extra scene for the play.
	One Hundred Years of Poetry for Children – Michael Harrison *Classic Poems for Children* – Nicola Baxter *New and Collected Poems for Children* – Carol Ann Duffy	*How to Train a Dragon* (series) – Cressida Cowell *Dragon Rider* – Cornelia Funke The *Dragonkeeper* trilogy – Carole Wilkinson *Working with Dragons* – Helen Ward *The Hobbit* – JRR Tolkien *Secret of the Sirens* – Julia Golding	*The Worst Thing About My Sister* – Jacqueline Wilson *Safy's Angel* – Hilary McKay *Journey to the River Sea* – Eva Ibbotson *The Family from One End Street* – Eve Garnett
	'Jeremy Strong biography and autobiography' 'Anthony Horowitz biography' (Biography and autobiography)	'The Kraken' 'A Dragon Spotter's Guide to the Chinese Lung Dragon' (Non-chronological reports)	'The Big Debate' (Discussion texts)
	Children examine the difference between biography and autobiography initially linked to material about Jeremy Strong. They use material about the author Anthony Horowitz to practise note-taking and plan an author blurb for a book. They adapt this into a biographical presentation about him, using PowerPoint or another presentation tool.	The non-fiction links to the *Dragon Slayer* story and introduces non-chronological reports through 'A field guide for ogre watchers'. Children explore the text type further by reading and deconstructing texts about the kraken and mythical dragons. They gather information about different dragons and then write their own field guide.	The non-fiction links to the fiction by exploring script forms such as broadcast scripts on non-fiction themes. Discussion texts are studied, looking at the conventions of oral debate. Children write a scripted speech and use it to debate whether junk food should be banned or not. They also write a discussion text.

Unit 1

Fiction: Myths
Non-fiction: Instructions

Timetable

WEEK 1 Reading fiction *Prometheus and Pandora*

Day 1	Day 2	Day 3	Day 4	Day 5
The story store	Word power 1 – synonyms	Word power 2	Re-read a story version 3	Who says?
Read a story version 1	Context	Special phrases	Grammar: cohesion within a paragraph	Dramatic reconstruction
Think and link	Read a story version 3	Re-read a story version 3	Who's the most important?	Daily log
Read a story version 2	Daily log	Clarify	What if not...?	Big Question
Daily log	Big Question	Daily log	Daily log	
Big Question		Big Question	Big Question	

WEEK 2 Writing fiction *Prometheus and Pandora*

Day 6	Day 7	Day 8	Day 9	Day 10
Build a sentence 🖶	Build a story 1	Write a story 1	Write a story 3	Evaluate and edit
Tell a story	Build a story 2	Write a story 2		Proofread
Daily log	Build a story 3 🖶	Daily log		Very Big Question
Big Question	Daily log 🖶	Big Question		
	Big Question			

WEEK 3 Reading and writing non-fiction Instructions

Day 11	Day 12	Day 13	Day 14	Day 15
Introduction	Deconstruction 1	Deconstruction 2 🖶	Deconstruction 3	Following instructions
Zoom in on instructions 🖶	Write an instructional text 1 🖶	Grammar: linking ideas across paragraphs	Write an instructional text 3*	Evaluate and edit
Instructional texts	Daily log	Write an instructional text 2	Proofread	
Audience		Daily log	Daily log	
Daily log				

*If you opt to *make* sherbet rather than watching the video, you will need to bring the ingredients to the lesson.

🖶: shows that a file should be printed out from the Software.

Overview of the Unit

In the Fiction section of this Unit the children will study the story of *Prometheus and Pandora*. It has been chosen for its strong mythological themes and characteristics. This version includes rich vocabulary and powerful imagery to convey the splendour of the gods and the struggles of the mortals.

Children will analyse the importance of different characters to the development of the story and the role of the narrator as storyteller. Differences between oral and written storytelling will also be explored and used to support the children's own storytelling and writing.

The Non-fiction section of the Unit will develop the children's understanding of the features of instructional writing. They will analyse, evaluate and write instructions. For more information about the Non-fiction week and the Non-fiction writing evaluation criteria, see p.37.

The Homework Book provides a homework activity related to the content of this Unit for each of the three weeks.

Fiction

Reading

Children will:

- make connections between the myth *Prometheus and Pandora*, other traditional tales and their own experiences
- understand that different characters are more important to the plot at different points in the story
- explore the narrator's point of view by looking at their description of characters' actions and their use of emotive language.

Writing

Key writing purpose to be shared with the children:

To write a new ending for Prometheus and Pandora *from Pandora's point of view, using ideas from the story and other traditional tales.*

Writing evaluation to be shared with the children

My new ending:

- *shows* my reader what Pandora is thinking and feeling through her actions
- builds suspense and vivid descriptions using interesting synonyms to engage the reader in Pandora's dilemma.

Grammar:

- is written in the first person and past tense to show the reader that I am narrating from Pandora's point of view
- includes conjunctions and adverbs to build cohesion within a paragraph.

See the Planning section of the Software ('Timetables' tab) for a printable version of the Writing purpose and evaluation.

Fiction: Myths
Prometheus and Pandora by Janey Pursglove

Resources
PB Pupils' Book, pp.4–14
A Anthology, pp.4–15
CD CD on interactive whiteboard, Unit 1
GB Grammar Bank on CD
HB Homework Book, pp.4–6

READING FICTION

DAY 1

Curriculum link: identifying and discussing themes and conventions, making comparisons within and across books

The story store (CD)

Purpose: *for children to develop an awareness of familiar and key elements of traditional stories*

- Explain that myths, legends and fairy tales helped people to understand things that happened in life and things that seemed unfair or hard to explain. They were not written down for many years so, to make the stories easy to remember and understand, they included very strong feelings, powerful characters, extreme actions and reactions. They used opposing forces of goodness/evil, power/weakness, love/hate to show how we think of ourselves, others, the world we know and sometimes worlds we don't know. Many stories have the same or similar elements.
- Use the **CD (file 1.1)** to show summaries of *Red Riding Hood, Sleeping Beauty* and *King Midas* to introduce children to some key elements in traditional stories. Read them to the children.
- Use the **CD (file 1.2)** to display the story grid, and click 'Complete' to show key elements common to all three stories (note all three answers for a row appear on one click).
- Tell the children they are now going to hear the bare bones of another myth and we are going to call it Story version 1.

read myths

Read a story version 1

Before the lesson, you may wish to watch the video demonstrating Read a story version 1 (with a Year 5 story). This can be found in the Extras section of the software.

Purpose: *for children to become familiar with Story version 1, the bare bones of the myth* Prometheus and Pandora

- Read Story version 1 aloud all the way through to the children. (Do not reveal any surprises or the ending of the final story.) Do not read the numbers aloud. The PowerPoint files open in a view which allows them to be edited. To take advantage of the full functionality of the files you should view them in Slide Show mode. Press F5 on the keyboard or select 'Slide Show' then 'View Show' from the PowerPoint toolbar.

  Story version 1
  1. By mistake, a young god makes some human beings.
  2. This makes the powerful king of the gods cross.
  3. The king of the gods punishes the human beings.
  4. This makes the young god angry with the king of the gods.
  5. He tries to trick the king of the gods.
  6. This makes the king of the gods *very* irritated.
  7. He punishes the young god and all of mankind for ever.
  8. The punishment involves a box, an attractive woman and the young god's brother.
- Use MT/YT (My turn/Your turn) and TTYP (Turn to your partner) for each point – you will need to break down the longer points! Use exaggerated intonation and emphasis where appropriate. This is to help the children to 'hold' the basic story in their heads.

Curriculum link: making comparisons, identifying themes

Think and link

Purpose: for children to make links and connections with other stories and their own experiences

- Now display Story version 1 on the **CD (file 1.3)**. Talk through each section, encouraging children to think about their own experiences and making connections with other stories they know.
- TOL (Think out loud): *'If I was king of the gods, why would I be angry when the young god made a human? Perhaps I was jealous because I hadn't made a human? Have you ever felt a little bit jealous when a friend has made something really special?*

  'Oh and when the young god is punished, that reminds me of the Sleeping Beauty story. Remember when the bad fairy punishes Sleeping Beauty's parents for not inviting them to the party?'

  'We know that the young god tries to trick the king of the gods. Can you think of any stories where someone tricks someone else? What about Red Riding Hood? Who plays tricks on her in that story? Have you ever tricked someone or been tricked yourself?'

  'What about the box? How could a box be part of a punishment? What might be in that box? I wonder if it was a gift that turns out to be something nasty. Which of the stories we talked about involve gifts? Were any of them not as great as they seemed to be?'

- Use TTYP and feedback to allow children to articulate and share ideas/connections and for you to paraphrase, clarify and extend their thoughts and ideas.

predicting; identifying how language, structure, and presentation contribute to meaning

Read a story version 2

Purpose: for children to examine how Story version 2 provides additional information for the reader and for the children to become more familiar with the story before they hear the full version

- Read Story version 2 aloud to the children.

  Story version 2

  1. A young god called Prometheus plays with some clay and accidentally makes some human beings.
  2. Zeus, the powerful king of the gods, is annoyed because Prometheus didn't have permission to make human beings.
  3. Prometheus watches over the humans and is kind to them.
  4. Zeus is jealous and outraged. He punishes the human beings even though they have done nothing wrong.
  5. Prometheus is furious with Zeus for being unfair and feels sorry for the humans. He tries to fool the king of the gods.
  6. The king of the gods is livid with Prometheus and wants to teach him a lesson.
  7. Zeus shows his fury and his power by ordering a terrible punishment for Prometheus.
  8. He also punishes all of mankind for evermore.
  9. He has a box made that contains a secret. He gives the box to a beautiful woman called Pandora and introduces her to the brother of Prometheus.
  10. Zeus uses Pandora and her box to punish the whole world without end.

- Re-read it, stopping after each section to ask the children if there are any words that tell them more about the people and the story. Ask children to TTYP and feed back.
- Now display this version on the **CD (file 1.4)**. Talk through the differences and then click 'Highlights' to identify the additional information:
  - addition of the words *jealous* and *unfair* to the description of Zeus
  - addition of the fact that the king of the gods *wants to teach him* (Prometheus) *a lesson*

- addition of the adjective *terrible* to describe the punishment
- addition of the fact that the box contains a *secret*
- we know characters' names – *Zeus, Prometheus, Pandora.*
- TOL and use TTYP to share how this extra information changes the pictures in our minds as we hear the story.

Curriculum link: noting and developing initial ideas

Daily log (CD)

Purpose: for children to be introduced to the process of keeping a personal log of notes, thoughts and ideas, collected from their reading and discussions, to use in their own writing

- Explain that many people make notes of their thoughts about things they see, hear, read and think about. Lots of writers do this and use the ideas in their own writing. They might collect cuttings and pictures, draw mind maps and diagrams, invent their own symbols as well as writing in prose. Explain that they are going to collect their thoughts and ideas in a Daily log. Show the children examples of Daily logs and mind maps on the **CD (file 1.5)**.
- Show the mind map of the story so far on the **CD (file 1.6)**. TOL about something of your own that you could add about the story so far, e.g. a symbol for a character or feeling.
- Ask the children to make their own mind map to record the story so far on the first plain page in their Daily log.

effective discussion; provide justifications for their views

Big Question (CD)

Purpose: for children to develop their skills of argument and discussion through a mini enquiry session based on a philosophical question relating to the work of the day

- Display today's Big Question on the **CD (file 1.7)**:

  Is getting angry ever a good thing?

- Ask the children to TTYP to discuss. Collect feedback from partners and scribe some responses. Tell the children that each day's Big Question and their thoughts will be put in a safe place until the end of Week 2. They will then vote on which question to discuss more deeply. See Introduction for further notes (p.13).

DAY 2

exploring the meaning of words in context

Word power 1 – synonyms (CD) (PB)

Purpose: for children to increase their knowledge of and application of synonyms and to examine how writers use language for effect

by mistake   accidently   cross   angry   outraged   furious   livid   annoyed
irritated   trick   fool   for ever   evermore   without end   attractive   beautiful

- Tell the children that there are lots different words in Story version 2 that mean the same as 'angry', 'cross' and 'irritated' in Story version 1. Tell them that these synonyms can show just *how* angry someone is.
- Display Story version 1 and Story version 2 on the **CD (file 2.1)** and click 'Show synonyms' to identify the synonyms for 'angry' – *cross, irritated, annoyed, outraged, livid, furious* (these are on screens 2 and 3).
- Write all of the 'angry' words (from Story versions 1 and 2) on cards and display on your Story wall.
- Navigate back through the screens and click 'Show synonyms' again to show other examples of synonymous words in both versions: *by mistake/accidentally, trick/fool, for ever/evermore/without end, attractive/beautiful.* Write on cards and add to your Story wall.

- TOL and use TTYP to share an example of how these words change the pictures in our minds as we hear the story. TTYP, asking the children to discuss other examples.
- Now tell the children to do the Word power 1 activity in the Pupils' Book p.4.

Curriculum link: discussing themes

Context

Purpose: for children to learn about the historical context for the story

- Explain that stories reflect how people looked and behaved in particular places and times. Explain that this story is set in Olympia, home to the gods of Ancient Greece. Navigate through **CD (file 2.2)** to show images of and facts about Ancient Greece, Olympia and myths.
- Re-read Story version 2 using the **CD (file 2.3)**. Focus on the section where Zeus punishes Prometheus for disobeying him (points 6 and 7). Ask children to TTYP to think of different types of punishments for particular wrongdoings, e.g. prison for murder, detention for not doing homework, grounded for being rude to your granny.
- Remind the children of examples of extreme punishments from the story summaries from Day 1, **CD (file 1.1)**, e.g. Red Riding Hood gets eaten by a wolf for not following instructions from her mother.
- TOL – '*We don't know what Zeus' punishment is yet but we can guess that it is going to be extreme.*' Explain to the children, 'You are Zeus. How are you going to punish Prometheus?' Ask children to TTYP and feed back. Paraphrase, talk about and show how valuable their ideas are.

explain and discuss their understanding of what they have read

Read a story version 3

Purpose: for children to hear and enjoy the full version of the story for the first time

- Tell the children they are now going to hear the whole story. Show your enthusiasm before you start. TOL about which parts *you* can't wait to hear about, etc.
- Read the full Story version 3 from the Anthology pp.4–11 to the children with great enjoyment, and appropriate intonation. Use exaggerated facial expressions and body language to add to your storytelling 'performance'!
- At the end of the story, ask the children to TTYP to discuss the questions in the Read a story version 3 activity in the Pupils' Book p.5. Then collect feedback.

Daily log

Purpose: for children to develop their thinking and recording skills by logging their initial response to the whole story

- Take one of the children's responses to one of the questions in the Read a story version 3 activity in the Pupils' Book p.5 and TOL as you model on the board how you could record this in note form in a Daily log, using different stem sentences: *'If I met Zeus I would...; I'd love the chance to meet Zeus so that I could...'*
- Explain that they are going to record at least one of the ideas they discussed with their partners. Tell them to TTYP to share what they are going to record. Ask them to say their opening sentence to their partner before writing it down.

effective discussion; provide justifications for their views

Big Question

Purpose: for children to develop their skills of argument and discussion through a mini enquiry session based on a philosophical question relating to the work of the day

- Display today's Big Question on the **CD (file 2.4)**:

  Do we all have power over something or somebody?

- Follow the process as explained at the end of Day 1 (p.24).

DAY 3

Word power 2 CD PB

Purpose: for children to learn the meaning of rarer vocabulary and discuss how these words and phrases are used in this story

Curriculum link: exploring the meaning of words in context

gargantuan potent appeased eternity bestowed upon exquisite distraught

- Display the Word power 2 words and their definitions on the **CD (file 3.1)**. Look at the words with the children and then read the sentences to them. Ask the children to repeat the sentences using MT/YT giving dramatic emphasis and actions as you say them.
- The children must hear, see and repeat the word in your teaching and conversation throughout the day: 'I have *bestowed upon* you my last pencil – I expect you to keep it for *eternity*!' Encourage the children to use the words at home with friends and family so that they become embedded in their own spoken (and eventually, written) vocabulary. Write the words on card and display on your Story wall.
- Now tell the children to do the Word power 2 activity in the Pupils' Book p.5.

Special phrases CD PB

exploring the meaning of words in context

Purpose: for children to become familiar with some special phrases particular to the story

For what is power without compassion?

The magnitude of your punishment will match my fury!

It was as if the sky's brightest and warmest sunbeam fell like drops of golden liquid onto his skin.

Let us rejoice in the life that we have.

Release us from our ceaseless toil

- Display the Special phrases from the story and their definitions on the **CD (file 3.2)**.
- Explain that you have chosen these because they are phrases that we don't use in our everyday talk and because they are linked to important moments in the story. Read the sentences and the definitions out loud. Say the phrases with obvious enjoyment, adding expression and intonation to show further meaning to the phrase.
- Now TOL (plan this ahead) as you draw attention to different features of some of the phrases that you like: similes, metaphors, rhythm of the words, sound of the words together, alliteration, sibilance, e.g.

  "Release us from our ceaseless toil." The way the words 'release us' and 'ceaseless' rhyme makes it sound like an echo coming from the box.'

  "What is power without compassion?" I think this is an important theme in the story. If you have power and don't care about people, you can go too far and do dreadful things.'

  "Prometheus, your punishment will match my fury!" This shows how just how angry Zeus is.

  "Let us be grateful for the life that we have." I like the bouncy rhythm of the first part of this – it matches the positive nature of the statement.'

  "It was as if warm sunbeams fell like golden liquid onto his skin." This is a simile to show the feeling of delight Pandora's beauty gave to Epimetheus.'
- Ask the children to TTYP to do the Special Phrases activity in the Pupils' Book p.6. Explain that some of the phrases have additional words or synonyms to the ones

in the Anthology. Ask them to search their Anthology text for the phrases, identify the differences and discuss which ones they prefer. Collect feedback.

- Have the Special phrases – you may add others you particularly like from the story – written on cards (before the lesson) and display them on your Story wall.

Curriculum link: checking that the book makes sense to them

Re-read a story version 3 A

Purpose: for children to gain a deeper understanding of the story and to see the text for the first time

- Let the children follow their own copy of the text in the Anthology pp.4–11 as you re-read the full version of the story aloud with great enthusiasm. Put special emphasis upon the Power words in bold.
- Now ask the children to read their copy of the story with their partners, alternate sections each, and to read the phrases in bold with great expression! Explain that you will be listening in.

explain and discuss their understanding of what they have read

Clarify A CD

Purpose: for children to clarify their understanding of the story

- Read one section of the story at a time, stopping after each section and thinking out loud to let the children 'see' your thought processes and understanding of the story. Tell them you are letting them see inside your mind as you read – as if you have a think bubble coming out of your head. Don't make it look too easy. Hesitate and ask yourself questions and answer them yourself. Bring the children into the TOL. Ask them to find the words and phrases you are talking about, but not as a Q and A session! See examples with text on the **CD (file 3.3)** and click 'TOL' to reveal thought bubbles.
- Occasionally ask the children to summarise a passage or find their favourite bit in a passage, using TTYP.

exploring the meaning of words in context

Daily log

Purpose: for children to keep a personal reading, writing and thinking log to record thoughts and ideas for their own writing

- Ask the children to decide on their favourite Word power words and/or Special phrases from the story and why they like them. Ask them to TTYP to share and then record in their Daily log.

effective discussion; provide justifications for their views

Big Question CD

Purpose: for children to develop their skills of argument and discussion through a mini enquiry session based on a philosophical question relating to the work of the day

- Display today's Big Question on the **CD (file 3.4)**:

  Have words got power?

- Follow the process as explained at the end of Day 1 (p.24).

DAY 4

read silently

Re-read a story version 3 A

Purpose: for children to deepen their understanding of a story by increasing familiarity with the text

- Ask the children to re-read the whole story silently from the Anthology pp.4–11. Tell them that they can stop to record any thoughts, ideas, questions and favourite bits in their Daily log as they read. Explain that it is more important for them to think about what they are reading than to finish first and, as they know the story, it doesn't matter if they don't finish this time.

Curriculum link: Year 5 Grammar
devices to build cohesion within a paragraph

Grammar: cohesion within a paragraph

Purpose: for children to develop their ability to recognise different devices that build cohesion within a paragraph

- Tell the children that you are going to explore a new word together and discover what it means. Explain that, as it is a tricky word, you are going to give them a clue about it first. Display **CD (file 4.1)**, showing just the first slide and the phrase 'sticking together'.
- Use MT/YT to read the phrase. Then ask the children to TTYP to talk about what this phrase means. Take feedback, drawing out that it can be used to mean sticking things together (like fixing something that has broken) but can also be to in the sense of people sticking together and being united (like friends or family).
- Now tell the children that you are going to show them the new word. Click to the next slide to display the word 'cohesion'. Explain that this is the tricky word that means 'sticking together' or 'something that fits together'. Use MT/YT to say the word out loud.
- To reinforce the idea of cohesion, ask a group of children to stand at the front. Explain that when you say 'cohesion' the children should huddle together tightly in a group, but when you say 'separation' the children should all move apart. Say each word a few times, ensuring the group at the front know how to react. Next, encourage the rest of the class to take turns to call out one of the words for the group to demonstrate.
- After the activity, explain that there are some words and phrases that are a bit like glue – they help ideas and other words to stick or link together, to give cohesion to a paragraph. Click to the next slide to show types of words that help make things link together in a text (you could use the term 'cohesive devices' if appropriate).
- Use MT/YT to read out each word. If appropriate, ask the children if they remember what these words mean, and whether they can think of any examples. Clarify if necessary.
- Progress to the next slide and use MT/YT to read out the word 'pronoun' and its meaning. Then focus on the example sentence and ask the children to TTYP to discuss which word they think is the pronoun in that sentence. Take feedback. Click 'Highlights' to highlight 'He' and to reveal the TOL bubble. Navigate through the slides repeating the process for 'conjunctions' and 'determiners'.
- Ask the children to look at the Grammar: building cohesion in a paragraph activity on p.6 of their Pupils' Book. Tell them to TTYP to complete the activity orally. Ask them to feedback their answers, clarifying where necessary.

Homework Book p.4 provides further practice on cohesion within a paragraph.

drawing inferences and justifying these with evidence

Who's the most important?

Purpose: for children to infer meaning from the text and to be able support their own views and ideas

- Tell the children that at different points in the story, different characters seem more important than others. Use the **CD (file 4.2)** to show one part of the story. Click 'TOL' to show the different points of view about which character might be the most important at that point in the story. Use TOL to add your own point of view. Make sure you use discursive language – *on the other hand, it could be that, another point of view could be* – as you try out ideas.
- Ask the children to look at the Who's the most important? activity in their Pupils' Book p.7 to explore who they think is the most important character in the whole story and why. Remind the children that there is no correct answer, just their own carefully considered opinions.

Curriculum link: drawing inferences and justifying with evidence, identifying key details that support ideas

What if not…? PB

Purpose: for children to consider how character, setting and plot affect each other

- Ask the children to look at the What if not…? questions in the Pupils' Book p.7. Model how you consider the first What if not…? What if not *powerful? What if* Zeus was *weak?*
- TOL: '*I suppose it would depend on when he lost his powers: if his power disappeared just as he took the fire away from earth, then the mortals would have been warm, safe, contented and the other gods wouldn't take any notice of him any more. On the other hand, the gods could have started fighting between themselves as to who would be in charge, and the mortals might have looked at the gods' lives and become dissatisfied. I wonder if Zeus would become kinder if he lost his awesome powers?*'
- Ask children to TTYP and discuss this and the other What if not…? questions in the Pupils' Book p.7. Collect feedback and encourage others to build upon argument. Give your opinion too.

Daily log

Purpose: for children to keep a personal reading, writing and thinking log to record thoughts and ideas for their own writing

- Ask the children to record at least one more What if not…? in their Daily log with some notes about how it would affect characters, plot or setting. Suggest they use mind maps to help them record their ideas simply.

effective discussion; provide justifications for their views

Big Question CD

Purpose: for children to develop their skills of argument and discussion through a mini enquiry session based on a philosophical question relating to the work of the day

- Display today's Big Question on the **CD (file 4.3):**

  Should every story have a happy ending?

- Follow the process explained at the end of Day 1 (p.24).

DAY 5

discuss and evaluate how authors use language, discuss viewpoints

Who says? CD A

Purpose: for children to develop their awareness of the narrative voice in a text

- Remind the children that the job of the narrator is to present the story in ways that the reader can understand. Display section 1 of the story on the **CD (file 5.1)**. Ask the children to re-read section 1 in the Anthology p.4 and then TTYP to answer: what information does the narrator give to the reader in this section?
- Collect feedback and scribe key points on the board.
- Tell the children that this narrator knows everything that has happened, but he wasn't involved himself. Our narrator is a bit like a witness to events.
- Explain that this time, we are not looking at *what* the narrator is telling us, but *how* he is telling us and what that might show us about his point of view. Show section 1 again on the **CD (file 5.1)**. Click 'Highlights' to identify emotive language that 'shows' his point of view.
- Ask the children to TTYP to discuss what these words and phrases show us about what the narrator might think of Zeus. Collect feedback.
- Explain that the narrator can also be a character in the story and so will tell the story from his/her own point of view in the first person. Now show the example of part of section 1 rewritten from Zeus' point of view on the **CD (file 5.2)**.
- TOL as you identify how Zeus makes sure the reader knows how powerful he is but also gets the reader to sympathise with his point of view before they even hear the whole story:

'...nothing I can't do if necessary... I do take my position very seriously though... punish those who disobey me or we would have everyone doing as they pleased...a foolish young god who dared to challenge my power...'

- Ask the children to read sections 7 and 8 of the story in the Anthology pp.9–11. Ask them to look at the information from the narrator. Ask: 'Do you think the narrator likes some characters more than others? How can you tell?'
- Ask for evidence to support their views. Encourage discussion, debate and opinions – not 'right' answers.

Curriculum link: consider different accounts of the same event and discuss viewpoints

Dramatic reconstruction PB

Purpose: *for children to empathise with particular characters; to go from words, to mind pictures to dramatic reconstruction; for children to become familiar with a scenario that could be used later for writing*

- Ask the children:
  - 'What do we know about Prometheus' character?' *(kind, brave, impetuous)*
  - 'How do we know?' Ask the children to TTYP. *(Feels responsible for the creatures he has created, doesn't always think about consequences of his actions – steals fire from Hephaistos, tries to bring comfort to the humans' lives, stands up to Zeus – tries to trick him to protect the humans.)*
- Ask the children:
  - 'What do we know about Zeus' character?' *(cruel, petty, has to be in control, jealous, easily offended, sneaky)*
  - 'How do we know?' Ask the children to TTYP. *(Enjoys the suffering of the humans and Prometheus. Punishes Prometheus for giving life to the humans even though it was an accident. Jealous because Prometheus cares about humans. His punishments are very harsh. Makes sure Pandora is so curious she will open the box. Makes the whole world suffer for the actions of a few.)*
- Put yourself in the role of Prometheus at the point in the story where he is about to be chained to the rock for eternity. Ask another adult or confident child to be Zeus. Brief them before the lesson, using the 'talking frame' below. Ask them to challenge and offer a counter argument to every defence that Prometheus gives for his behaviour.

  Prometheus asks half of the children, in role as humans, to support him in dealing with the very angry Zeus. Zeus asks the other half of the children, in role as gods of Olympus, to support him in dealing with the very frightened but determined Prometheus.

  The responses are suggestions only – use your own ideas and encourage the children to think 'in role' and respond as naturally as possible!

  Prometheus: Did I not always try to do the right thing for the humans? Am I not trustworthy and honourable?

  (Prometheus calls for the humans to call out in support of him and his actions: *Yes! You have always tried to do the right thing! It would be cruel to let the humans die!*)

  Zeus: Trustworthy? Honourable? What's honourable about disobeying the god of gods? The mighty Zeus!

  (You tell him Zeus! Thinks he's better than rest of us.)

  Prometheus: I never intended the creature I made to come to life. I tried to take responsibility for my actions!

(Yes, Yes! It wasn't your fault – you were just playing! One quick breath and they were alive! You had to try to look after the humans. You didn't mean to do it!)

Zeus: The breath of life is sacred and belongs only to me. Responsibility! Everyone has only one responsibility and that is to obey me!

Prometheus: You should have just punished me. Why must everyone suffer for my mistakes?

(You see! Prometheus is so noble and brave…and it does seem a bit unfair for everyone to be punished…we've not actually done anything wrong.)

Zeus: You pathetic weakling. How dare you question my decisions? Take care, supporters of Prometheus, or I will unleash more evils on the world!

(At this rate we'll all be chained up with our livers being eaten by eagles and we wouldn't even argue with you Zeus.)

- Now organise the class into fours – two sets of partners: Prometheus and Zeus, with one supporter for Prometheus and one supporter for Zeus. The children use the prompts in the Dramatic reconstruction activity in the Pupils' Book p.8 to keep their group on track. Ask them to act out one section of the role-play at a time!

Curriculum link: provide reasoned justifications for their views

Daily log

Purpose: for children to keep a personal reading, writing and thinking log to record thoughts and ideas for their own writing

- Ask the children to record in their Daily log which character they felt most empathy with, or sympathy for, and why.

effective discussion; provide justifications for their views

Big Question (CD)

Purpose: for children to develop their skills of argument and discussion through a mini enquiry session based on a philosophical question relating to the work of the day

- Display today's Big Question on the **CD (file 5.3):**

  Is life one big story?

- Follow the process explained at the end of Day 1 (p.24).

WRITING FICTION

DAY 6

describing settings, characters and atmosphere

Build a sentence (CD) (PB)

Purpose: for children to build a sentence around one Power word, deepening the meaning of the word

- Use the **CD (file 6.1)** to show the part of the story where 'faltering' is used:
- 'As if to guide her *faltering* hand and heart, from within the chest came the sound of many voices, singing in harmonies that were enchanting and yet full of sorrow.'

  Read it aloud. Explain that you really like the word 'faltering' here. Say the sentence again and mime the action of 'faltering' as you say it. Tell the children that you have used a thesaurus to find synonyms for this word. Click 'Synonyms' to show these words: *uncertain, unsure, hesitant, tentative, cautious, undecided.*

- Keep re-reading the sentence substituting synonyms for 'faltering'. Ask the children which one sounds best. Do any of them sound better than 'faltering'?

- TOL: '*What if I wanted to start a sentence with "faltering". Would it work? Let's see…*' Ask for examples of situations where someone might move and act in a faltering manner. TOL offering a few ideas and then ask the children to TTYP to share some ideas of their own, e.g. handling a pet for the first time, walking around in the dark.
- Now use these prompts to model the thinking and planning process. Begin with a sentence starting with the word 'Faltering'. TOL as you try different ideas – don't write straight away.

  'Who might be walking around in the dark? Who could we have? A frail old man who is looking for the light switch on the wall? A woman taking shelter?'

  'What sort of house? A grand house on a city street, a tiny cottage in the country, an abandoned house?'
- Perhaps you like the idea of a woman taking shelter in an abandoned house. Don't write straight away. Say the sentence.
  'Faltering, she stepped into the abandoned house.'
- Ask the children to say the sentence using MT/YT and then write it on a flipchart. Continue to use the prompts below as you now TOL and model the *writing* process. It is important to let the children see writing in action and the prompts may be printed off the **CD (file 6.2)** for you to use as a script. TOL:
  - '*Why is she there, in an abandoned house? Perhaps she is taking shelter because she's cold? TTYP and show each other that you are cold. Let's think of some words that show that someone is cold: shivering, huddled, freezing, perishing. I like the word "shivering":*
    "Faltering, the shivering woman stepped into the abandoned house."'
  - '*What could our abandoned house look like? It has been empty for years so is it dusty? What else would be in the house? What would not be in the house?*
    "Faltering, the woman shivered as she stepped into the empty, dusty abandoned house."'
  - '*Shall we move the words around to see if it sounds better?*
    "Faltering, the woman shivered as she stepped into the empty, abandoned house the dusty…"'
  - '*Now we'll have to add some punctuation and perhaps have two sentences.*
    "Faltering, the woman shivered as she stepped into the empty, abandoned house. The dusty…"'
  - '*Which part of the house would she be in if she had just stepped in?*
    "Faltering, the woman shivered as she stepped into the empty, abandoned house. The dusty hallway was…"'
  - '*I think I'll add some cobwebs and a mouse.*
    "Faltering, the woman shivered as she stepped into the empty, abandoned house. The dusty hallway was full of cobwebs and a mouse ran across the floor."'
  - 'Let's picture the mouse as it ran across the floor. What is a more powerful word than "ran" that fits with a mouse? Do a mime with your fingers to show a mouse running up your arm. TTYP to think of some synonyms. We could have: scooted, scuttled, scurried, scampered, dashed, darted.
    "Faltering, the woman shivered as she stepped into the empty, abandoned house. The dusty hallway was full of cobwebs and a mouse ***scurried*** *across the floor."*'
- Hide your sentence. Ask the children, either individually or as partners, to compose their own sentence out loud using the prompts in the Build a sentence activity in the Pupils' Book p.9. Do not let them write until they can say their sentence out loud. Ask partners to take turns to develop each other's sentences. Encourage crossings out, switching words round, etc. Emphasise that this is writing in action – it is not a neat, finished piece of writing!

Curriculum link: consider different accounts of the same event

Tell a story

Purpose: for children to develop their awareness of the differences between oral and written stories; for children to develop confidence in building a story orally

- Remind children that many stories were spoken and not written down for many years. This is why we often have lots of slightly different versions of the same story – as they were retold each person would forget, change or add a bit while keeping the basic story.
- Now use the **CD (file 6.3)** to show the extended version of the sentences used in the Build a sentence activity. Read it to the children.
- Explain that you are going to have a go at retelling the story to them without looking at the written text (prepare your retelling before the lesson). Ask them to listen carefully for:
  - missing information
  - additional information
  - how the order of the story might be different
  - more everyday language
  - use of body language, facial expressions to emphasise and engage the audience, etc.
- Ask the children to TTYP to share what differences they noticed. They will need to refer to the written version of the original text in the Tell a story activity in the Pupils' Book p.9. Collect feedback.
- Now use the **CD (file 6.4)** to play the audio version of another oral retelling of the story so far. Then show the transcripts of the oral version and the original written version on the **CD (file 6.5)** for comparison. Use the highlighter tool on you whiteboard as you talk through the differences between them.
- Tell the children that they are going re-read the story so far in the Pupils' Book p.9 and then develop the story orally with their partners. They should swap roles from teller to listener and vice versa when you say *stop and swap* at about 30 second intervals (two or three times), continuing the story from that point each time. Emphasis should be on building confidence in storytelling and keeping their audience engaged!

noting initial ideas

Daily log

Purpose: for children to keep a personal reading, writing and thinking log to record thoughts and ideas for their own writing

- Ask the children to write down one of the ideas they discussed with their partner for continuing the story.

effective discussion; provide justifications for their views

Big Question

Purpose: for children to develop their skills of argument and discussion through a mini enquiry session based on a philosophical question relating to the work of the day

- Display today's Big Question on the **CD (file 6.6)**:

  Are stories important?

- Follow the process as explained at the end of Day 1 (p.24).

DAY 7

understand, through being shown, the processes essential for writing

Build a story 1

Purpose: for children to be able to see a story grow through three stages of development

- Remind the children that they heard two versions of *Prometheus and Pandora* (Story versions 1 and 2) before they heard and read the full story. It *prepared* them to *read* the full story.

- Explain that you are going to show them two versions of a new story to be written. These versions *prepared* the writer to *write* the full story. Show the Build a story 1 – questions on the **CD (file 7.1)** and explain that these were the questions that helped the writer to know what to put in the new story. You are in role as writer of the story during these activities.
- Now display Build a story 1 on the **CD (file 7.2)**.
- Read out loud to the children. Explain that you are now going to show them another version of the new story to be written. This one has additional information – it has been developed.

Curriculum link: consider how authors have developed characters and settings

Build a story 2 (CD)

Purpose: for children to be able to see a story grow through three stages of development

- Show Build a story 2 on the **CD (file 7.3)**. TOL as you compare this version with Build a Story 1. Click 'Highlights' to show additional information.
- Draw children's attention to the devices that build cohesion that they looked at on Day 4 – conjunctions (so), pronouns (He) and determiners (this).

Build a story 3 (CD) (PB)

Purpose: for the children to see an example of writing that will provide a model for their own writing

- An example story is provided as a model for writing. Remain in role as the writer of this story during these activities.
- Display the story on the **CD (file 7.5)**. Explain that when writing this story, you were in the role of the first human that Prometheus made and sent to earth. Read 'your' story (Build a story 3) to the children.
- Print out a copy of the story, from **CD (file 7.4)** for each set of partners. Using TTYP and oral feedback, ask the children to evaluate the writing using the guide questions in the Build a story 3 activity in the Pupils' Book p.10.

noting ideas

Daily log (CD)

Purpose: for children to keep a personal reading, writing and thinking log to record thoughts and ideas for their own writing

- Ask the children to take turns to read a section each of Build a story 3, printed from the **CD (file 7.4),** and then share ideas for a title for the story. Ask them to record their best idea in their Daily log and explain why they think it is a good title.

effective discussion; provide justifications for their views

Big Question (CD)

Purpose: for children to develop their skills of argument and discussion through a mini enquiry session based on a philosophical question relating to the work of the day

- Display today's Big Question on the **CD (file 7.6)**:

  Is there always hope in any situation?

- Follow the process as explained at the end of Day 1 (p.24).

DAY 8

understand through being shown the processes essential for writing

Write a story 1 (A) (CD)

Purpose: to develop children's confidence and skills in story planning and development

- Tell the children they are going to write a story in the role of Pandora. Ask them to find sections 7 and 8 of the story in the Anthology pp.9–11 and follow as you read aloud, to remind themselves of her part in the story.

- Remind the children of when they took on the roles as Zeus and Prometheus (Dramatic reconstruction). Tell them that Partner 1 is now Pandora and Partner 2 is now Epimetheus and they are going to have a discussion about the mysterious box. Use these guide questions to stimulate a short role-play:

  Walk around and listen in:

  – Which one of you wants to open the box? Why?
  – What do you think might be in it?
  – Do you think anyone will know if you open it?
- Give feedback on good discussions.
- Now show the children the pre-prepared 'bare bones' version of Pandora's story on the **CD (file 8.1)** for the children to read.

Curriculum link: describing characters and atmosphere

Write a story 2 PB CD

Purpose: for children to develop confidence and skills in story planning and development

- Still displaying **CD (file 8.1)** and using TOL, and encouraging the children to offer their ideas, model how to develop sentence 1 by adding some information and phrases and changing some words. Write on a flipchart or large sheet of paper.
- Repeat using sentence 2.
- Ask the children to develop sentence 3 using the prompts in the Pupils' Book p.11. Tell them to compose individually their sentence in their heads first. They must make sure they can say their opening sentence to their partner before they start to write.
- Explain that sentence 4 has already been developed. Display the developed version of sentence 4 on the **CD (file 8.2)**. Guide children to identify features that show the development.
- Ask the children to develop sentence 5 using the prompts in the Write a story 2 activity in the Pupils' Book p.11 in the same way as they did for sentence 3.

noting ideas

Daily log

Purpose: for children to keep a personal reading, writing and thinking log to record thoughts and ideas for their own writing

- Ask the children to write at least three pieces of advice to someone about how to write a story.

effective discussion; provide justifications for their views

Big Question CD

Purpose: for children to develop their skills of argument and discussion through a mini enquiry session based on a philosophical question relating to the work of the day

- Display today's Big Question on the **CD (file 8.3)**:

  Should we always do exactly as we are told?*
- Follow the process as explained at the end of Day 1 (p.24).

**This Big Question will be revisited on Day 11 – the first day of the Non-fiction week.*

DAY 9

describing characters and atmosphere

Write a story 3 PB

Purpose: for children to use the sentences they have already developed to write their full, first person narrative version of Pandora's story

- Tell the children that they are ready to write their own story from Pandora's point of view. Ask them to continue to refer to the prompts in the Pupils' Book p.11 (Write a story 2). Remind them to use any useful parts of their Daily log to help them and to look at the Story wall for Power words and phrases and a thesaurus for synonyms.

- Encourage children to rehearse their opening sentence with their partners before they begin to write.

DAY 10

Curriculum link: assessing the effectiveness of their own and others' writing

Evaluate and edit (CD)

Purpose: for children to evaluate their own and their partner's work against specific criteria and then discuss how they could improve their work

- Display **CD (file 10.1)** to show the evaluation prompts and read them together using MT/YT.
- As a model, select an example of work from the children where the writing has met the criteria, and share this with the other children, explaining why it works well.
- Tell the children to take turns to read their partner's writing and discuss how well they have met the criteria.
- Ask children to discuss at least two changes they could make to improve their work following the partner discussion.

proofread for spelling and punctuation errors

Proofread

Purpose: for children to proofread their work and make changes to improve the accuracy of their grammar, punctuation and spelling

- Now ask the children to proofread their work. If you have noticed that several children need to improve on a particular aspect of spelling, grammar or punctuation, use this as a focus for the Proofread activity. Write an example which includes common errors from the children's writing and use this as a model.
- The children should always be checking for standard use of punctuation and correct spelling of common exception words.
- The following points would be relevant as the particular focus for this Unit:
  - checking that speech is punctuated correctly
  - checking that capital letters are used for proper nouns
  - checking there is cohesion within a paragraph.

effective discussion; provide justifications for their views, distinguish between fact and opinion

Very Big Question (CD)

Purpose: for children to develop or revise their opinions through the exploration of one of the Big Questions in more depth

- Explain to the children that they are going to vote to choose one of the Big Questions they have discussed to explore further in this lesson.
- Tell the children the 'rules' for the Very Big Question time:

  Think before you talk. Wait for others to finish before you talk. Good listening.

- Display the Big Question they have voted for on the CD (choose from the Big Questions debated so far in the Unit – these are all listed on the Day 10 lesson plan on the Software). Give everyone some time to think about the question. Ask partners to share their thoughts on the question.
- Allow each child to express their opinion. Encourage responses from children to what has been said rather than insisting that each child speaks in turn. Step in to clarify, paraphrase or draw in children who are reluctant to talk.
- As the 'enquiry' develops and changes direction, pause the proceedings occasionally and re-frame the question – remember the Big Question is a starting point for genuine enquiry. Repeat thinking time and TTYP to refresh the process and to prevent one or two children dominating.
- Allow time to have a final round where children are asked to think about what has been said and share how their opinion has changed or not as a result of the discussion.

Instructions

READING AND WRITING NON-FICTION

The non-fiction part of the Unit develops children's understanding of the features of instructional writing. They will analyse, evaluate and write instructions. The outcome is for children to write instructions for making sherbet, which are followed and evaluated by their peers.

See p.20 for the daily timetable for the Non-fiction week.

Non-fiction

Reading

Children will:

- learn how instructions are organised to make them easy to follow
- identify key features of instruction texts
- consider the audience and purpose of different instruction texts.

Writing

Key writing purpose to be shared with the children:

To write a clear set of instructions explaining how to make lemon sherbet.

Writing evaluation to be shared with the children

My instructions:

- include all the important information from my notes about how to make lemon sherbet
- are clear and accurate so the reader can make sherbet successfully
- are easy to follow because I have used organisational features of instructions, e.g. *pictures, diagrams, text boxes, numbering.*

Grammar:

- includes adverbs of time (*Next, Then*) to link ideas within the instructions, so they are easy to follow.

See the Planning section of the Software ('Timetables' tab) for a printable version of the Writing purpose and evaluation.

DAY 11

Curriculum link: learn the conventions of different types of writing

Introduction

Purpose: for children to revise their existing knowledge of instructional texts using the context of one of the Big Questions and the fiction text studied in Weeks 1 and 2

- Show the Big Question from Day 8: *Should we always do exactly as we are told?* on the **CD (file 8.3).**
- Ask the children to TTYP to recall some of the reasons they gave in favour of always doing as we are told and following instructions. Collect feedback.
- Remind the children that in the myth of *Prometheus and Pandora* from Weeks 1 and 2, Pandora was given a very simple *instruction* that she ignored with terrible consequences. Ask the children to TTYP to remind each other what instruction she was given about the box. Read this section of the story out loud from the Anthology p.10, giving greater emphasis to the words that are highlighted:

  Now, as well as her many qualities, Pandora brought with her a box, which ***Zeus commanded her never, ever to open.*** Epimetheus also urged Pandora to obey the gods and never open the mysterious casket.

- Explain that this is a very simple instruction telling someone not to do something and we all spend a lot of time following or being given instructions which can be telling us what not to do or what to do. TOL as you model some examples:

  'This morning when I got to school, a rubbish collector stopped me and said, "Don't park your car too close to my truck please!"'

  'Oh and when I saw a pupil throw a sweet wrapper down on the playground, I said, "Please pick that up immediately!"'

- Ask the children to TTYP to think of a simple instruction that they have given or been given today. Collect feedback.
- Explain that these simple instructions could have additional information or advice. Read these examples out loud or make up your own:

  "Don't park your car too close to my truck please. *There is a better parking space by the gate*."

  "Please pick that up immediately! *Now put it in the bin over there!*"

  Pandora brought with her a box, which Zeus commanded her never, ever to open *because it contained something that should never be set free.*

- Explain that extra information is sometimes needed to make sure we understand the instructions and to make us more likely to follow them. Perhaps Pandora would not have ignored the instruction about the box if she had been given more information!
- Tell the children that more complicated instructions are usually written down to make them easier to remember and follow.
- Say that a set of instructions that should have been attached to Pandora's box has been found. Display these on the **CD (file 11.1)**.
- Then ask them to discuss with their partner: Would these instructions have stopped Pandora opening the box?
- Collect feedback. Explain that:
  - once we write something down it is called a text
  - written instructions have certain features that make them easy to follow and understand

- if we forget what to do, we can refer back to instructions if they are written down
- the instructions for Pandora is one example of an *instructional text*.

- Ask the children to TTYP to think of different types of instructions that are usually written down.

Curriculum link: exploring the meaning of words in context

Zoom in on instructions

Purpose: for children to become familiar with some words associated with instructional texts

instructions *procedure* *sequence* *adverbs of time*

- Display the words and their definitions on the **CD (file 11.2)**. Look at them with the children and read each sentence to the children. Ask them to repeat the sentences using MT/YT.
- Find opportunities to use the words yourself during the day, e.g. 'Oh dear, my *instructions* were not very clear were they?' 'Who can remember the *procedure* for going into assembly?' and encourage the children to use them in their everyday conversation.

  Large versions of the words can be printed off from the **CD (file 11.3)** to display on your Non-fiction wall.
- Now tell the children to do the Zoom in on instructions activity in the Pupils' Book p.12.

information retrieval

Instructional texts

Purpose: for children to be able to recognise the basic structure and features of instructional texts

- Display the extracts from different instructional texts on the **CD (file 11.4).**
- Read each text out loud to the children. Ask them to look at the texts in the Pupils' Book p.13 (A–D) and TTYP to discuss how they could tell they were sets of instructions. Collect feedback.
- Then click 'Key features' on the CD to display them. Using the highlighter tool on your whiteboard highlight examples of the features in the instructional texts.

identifying the audience and purpose

Audience

Purpose: for children to be able to recognise that the basic structure and language of instructional texts will vary to suit different audiences and purposes

- Display the extracts from the instructional texts again on the **CD (file 11.4)**. TOL as you spot clues that help you to identify the probable purpose and target audience (reader) of text A. Use these prompts if you need to:
- TOL: '*Hmm, this seems to be instructions for something like flat-pack furniture because… Oh and it mentions using a "standard or electric screwdriver" so I'm sure these instructions aren't meant for…and the language is very plain with no chatty bits so I think the audience is most likely…*'
- Now ask the children to look at the texts and list of possible audiences in the Instructional texts activity in the Pupils' Book pp.12–13. Tell them to TTYP to discuss and then choose the probable audience of the other texts (e.g. teenager = text B? C? D?). Remind them that they should explain their choices.

Curriculum link: noting initial ideas, drawing on reading and research

Daily log

Purpose: for children to keep a personal reading, writing and thinking log to record thoughts and ideas for their own writing

- Tell the children that over the next few days, you want them to look in magazines, newspapers, the Internet, and on packaging for written instructions of any kind to bring in to stick in their Daily log. Tell them to write a note next to each one of where they found it.

DAY 12

plan their writing, retrieve information from non-fiction

Deconstruction 1

Purpose: for children to see an example of writing that will provide a model for the planning of their own writing

- Ask the children to find the 'How to Write Instructions' text in the Anthology p.12. Tell them to follow the text as you read it aloud with lots of expression.
- Explain that this text will be used as a reference to help them to plan their own set of instructions. Ask them to TTYP and read the text, reading alternate sections each.
- Now ask the children to TTYP to decide which parts of these instructions were the most helpful. Take feedback and encourage further analysis and discussion.

identifying the audience for and purpose of the writing, developing initial ideas

Write an instructional text 1

Purpose: for children to develop their confidence and skills in planning an instructional text

- Ask the children to look in their Daily log to find the three pieces of advice they wrote for someone who was about to write a story (see Day 8, Daily log activity).
- Explain that they are going to develop these into a plan for a set of instructions on how to write a good story.The instructions will be for a Year 4 pupil. Display the planning grid on the **CD (file 12.2)** and TOL to explain how the children should fill in their own grids. Click 'Complete' to show example entries for the first two rows.
- Give each child a printed copy of of the plan, from the **CD (file 12.1)**. Ask the children to fill in their own grids and to include their three pieces of advice. Walk around as they are working, noting good examples to share during the feedback session. Allow time for partners to share their ideas before asking for feedback.

retrieve and record information

Daily log

Purpose: for children to keep a personal reading, writing and thinking log in order to record thoughts and ideas for their own writing

- Ask the children to choose their favourite bit of advice or information from the 'How to Write Instructions' text in the Anthology p.12 and copy it in their Daily log. Tell them to add a few sentences explaining what they like about it

DAY 13

plan their writing, using similar writing as models for their own

Deconstruction 2

Purpose: for children to see an example of writing that will provide a model for their own writing

- Tell the children that they are already experts on the Greek myth of *Prometheus and Pandora* but you have found some *instructions* that explain how to *write* a Greek myth in the Anthology p.13. Tell them to follow the text as you read it out loud with lots of expression.
- Then ask the children to read it with their partners, reading alternate sections each.
- Display printable **CD (file 13.1)** to show the key features checklist grid. Explain the two examples given.

- Give the children a copy each of the grid to complete. Tell them to work with their partners and the Anthology text p.13 to find examples of the features listed.
- Collect examples from partners and clarify points where necessary.

Curriculum link: Year 5 Grammar
linking ideas across paragraphs

Grammar: linking ideas across paragraphs

Purpose: for children to develop ability to recognise how ideas can link across paragraphs using adverbs and adverbials

- Display the **CD (file 13.2)** to show the word *cohesion*. Remind the children that they explored this word earlier in this unit (Day 4). Ask them to TTYP to talk about what it means then take feedback. If necessary, emphasise that it means 'sticking together' or 'something that fits together'. Remind the children how *pronouns, conjunctions* and *determiners* can help to build cohesion within a paragraph.
- Explain that this word 'cohesion' can also refer to the way different paragraphs are linked together in a text. For example, in instruction texts, adverbs of time such as *first, next, then* and *finally* can start new paragraphs, showing the order in which things need to be done.
- Click to the next slide and explain that it shows part of an instruction text that they looked at earlier. Ask the children to TTYP to talk about which words are adverbs of time that link the paragraphs together. Take feedback, then click 'Highlights' to reveal the adverbs *First, Next* and *Finally*. Explain that the red arrows show links (*cohesion*) between the paragraphs.
- Tell the children that as well as using adverbs of time to link paragraphs, you can also use adverbs of place, such as *nearby, underneath, close to*. Remind them that sometimes a group of words make up an 'adverbial' which is a group of words that act like an adverb, e.g. *at the tree, down in the field*.
- Click to the next slide and ask children to TTYP to talk about which words are adverbs (or adverbials) of place. Take feedback, then click 'Highlights' to reveal the appropriate adverbs and adverbials. Again, point out that the red arrows show links (cohesion) between the paragraphs.
- Ask the children to look at the Grammar: linking ideas across paragraphs activity on p.14 of their Pupils' Book. Tell them to TTYP to complete the activity orally. Ask them to feedback their answers, clarifying where necessary. They should identify *First* and *Finally* as adverbs of time, and *At the far shore* as an adverbial showing place.

Homework Book p.6 provides further practice on linking ideas across paragraphs.

plan their writing by using similar writing as models for their own

Write an instructional text 2

Purpose: for children to use their planning grid to help them to write a full length instructional text

- Remind the children that on Day 12 they completed a planning grid for a set of instructions for Year 4 pupils on how to write a good story.
- Explain that you have used the grid to help to begin your own instructional text. Display the **CD (file 13.3)** clicking 'Complete' to fill in each section of the grid.
- Now display the **CD (file 13.4)** to show 'your' text. Click 'TOL' to display the think bubbles to explain how the planning grid helped you organise your instructions clearly.
- Point out how the use of adverbs of time will provide cohesion, or links, in the instructions.
- Tell the children that they are now ready to write a set of instructions using their own completed planning grids.

- Remind them to:
  - use any useful parts of their Daily log
  - look at the 'How to Write Instructions' text in the Anthology p.12
  - use a thesaurus for synonyms.
- Encourage the children to rehearse their opening sentence with their partners before they write.
- Make sure you have the ingredients for making home-made sherbet for Day 14 – see **CD (file 14.2)**. Citric acid in powdered form is available from most high street chemists.

Curriculum link: noting initial ideas

Daily log

Purpose: for children to keep a personal reading, writing and thinking log to record thoughts and ideas for their own writing

- Tell the children a really good piece of advice you have heard, e.g. make sure you laugh every day. Ask them to TTYP to discuss what the best piece of advice is that they have ever heard. Tell them to write theirs and their partner's best advice in their Daily log.

DAY 14

assessing the effectiveness of others' writing

Deconstruction 3 A PB

Purpose: for children to see an example of writing for them to evaluate the effectiveness of layout, organisation and clarity

- Tell the children one of the most common forms of instructional texts is the recipe. Ask them to follow the recipe for home-made ice cream in the Anthology pp.14–15 as you read it aloud with lots of expression.
- Now ask them to take turns to read it to each other one section at a time. Explain that:
  - The writer was very keen for people to try out his recipe and so he wanted it to stand out and look more interesting than the many other recipes for home-made ice cream.
  - He was also fascinated by facts about ice cream and added those as well!
  - He chose to display his instructions and extra information using page design techniques. We call this the *layout* and *organisation* of the information on the page.
- Ask the children to use the prompts in the Ice cream recipe activity in the Pupils' Book p.14 to identify how effectively the instructions are displayed.
- Collect feedback and collate evaluation scores.

drafting, developing ideas

Write an instructional text 3 CD

Purpose: for children to write a recipe for others to try out

- Explain to the children that you are going to show a video of someone making home-made sherbet (or demonstrate yourself if you prefer). Tell them to watch and listen carefully. Show the video on **CD (file 14.1)** or demonstrate it yourself using the recipe on the **CD (file 14.2)**.
- Tell the children that you are going to show the video or run through the process again and this time you want them to make notes on the equipment needed, the ingredients and the method.
- Ask them to TTYP to share their notes and then join another pair. Once in their groups of four, tell the children to share and pool their information.
- Explain that their task is to work together to write a set of clear instructions on how to make home-made sherbet and how to adjust the recipe to get the right levels of sweetness and fizziness.

- Tell them that their instructions will be used by another group tomorrow to make sherbet and a 'taste test' will help them to evaluate the success of the instructions. At the end of the lesson collect in the instructions from each group.

Curriculum link: proofread for spelling and punctuation errors

Proofread

Purpose: for children to proofread their work and make changes to improve the accuracy of their grammar, punctuation and spelling

- Now ask the children to proofread their work. If you have noticed that several children need to improve on a particular aspect of spelling, grammar or punctuation, use this as a focus for the Proofread activity. Write an example which includes common errors from the children's writing and use this as a model.
- The children should always be checking for standard use of punctuation and correct spelling of common exception words.
- The following points would be relevant as the particular focus for this Unit:
  – checking that instructions make sense and are correctly sequenced
  – checking for correct use of adverbs of time, e.g. *next, then*, to link ideas across paragraphs
  – checking for correct use of punctuation.

Daily log

Purpose: for children to keep a personal reading, writing and thinking log to record thoughts and ideas for their own writing

- Ask the children to think about how they felt working in a small group to write their instructions. Ask them to record two things they didn't like or find easy and two things they did like or they thought made the task easier.

DAY 15

Following instructions

Purpose: for children to follow a recipe and to evaluate its success

- Put out a set of ingredients and equipment per table of four.
- Divide the recipes between the groups ensuring that no group has their own recipe. Tell the children that they are to work as a team to follow the recipe they have *exactly* – even if they think it is wrong!
- Remind them that they are going to be evaluating the usefulness and clarity of the instructions as well as the taste of the sherbet.

assessing the effectiveness of their own and others' writing

Evaluate and edit

Purpose: for children to evaluate their own and their partner's work against specific criteria and then discuss how they could improve their work

- Display **CD (file 15.1)** to show the evaluation prompts and read them together using MT/YT.
- As a model, select an example of work from the children where the writing has met the criteria, and share this with the other children, explaining why it works well.
- Tell the children to take turns to read their partner's writing and discuss how well they have met the criteria.
- Ask children to discuss at least two changes they could make to improve their work following the partner discussion.

Fiction: A modern retelling of a myth/ dilemma story
Non-Fiction: Recounts

Timetable

WEEK 1 Reading fiction *Bling!*

Day 1	Day 2	Day 3	Day 4	Day 5
The story store	Read a story version 3	Word power 🖶	Re-read a story version 3	Consequences
Read a story version 1	Context 🖶	Re-read a story version 3	Special phrases 🖶	What if not…?
Think and link	Map the story	Clarify	Word play	Daily log
Read a story version 2	Daily log	Grammar: relative clauses 1	Drama – status game	Drama – hotseating
Daily log – understanding a character	Big Question	Daily log – Images	Daily log – synonyms	Big Question
Big Question		Big Question	Big Question	

WEEK 2 Writing fiction *Bling!*

Day 6	Day 7	Day 8	Day 9	Day 10
Build a sentence 🖶	Build a character	Dilemma drama	Write a story 3	Share a story
Tell a story	Daily log	Write a story 1		Evaluate and edit
Daily log	Build a story ending 1	Write a story 2		Proofread
Big Question	Build a story ending 2 🖶	Daily log		Very Big Question
	Daily log 🖶	Big Question		
	Big Question			

WEEK 3 Reading and writing non-fiction Recounts

Day 11	Day 12	Day 13	Day 14	Day 15
Linking the texts	Deconstruction 1	Deconstruction 2	Deconstruction 3 – evaluate layout	Evaluate and edit
Introduction	Read a recount 🖶	Grammar: relative clauses 2	Write a recount	Proofread
Points of view		Build a recount 🖶	Daily log	
Zoom in on recounts		Daily log		
Daily log				

🖶: shows that a file should be printed out from the Software.

Overview of the Unit

This Unit uses the story *Bling!* (a modern retelling of the King Midas myth) to focus on how a dilemma can be the driving force of a narrative. The children will pick apart the dilemma, explore the writer's craft in creating characters of different status and empathise with the main character's dilemma. The outcome of the fiction will be for the children to compose an ending to the story through writing a diary entry in role as the character Billy.

The Non-fiction section links to this through exploring the difference in a first person recount such as a diary and a newspaper report of the same event. For more information about the Non-fiction week and the Non-fiction writing evaluation criteria, see p.60.

The Homework Book provides a homework activity related to the content of this Unit for each of the three weeks.

Fiction

Reading

Children will:

- learn about the concept of a dilemma, and engage with the dilemma in *Bling!*
- make links between their own experiences and stories they have read
- explore how Billy's choices change the way he behaves towards other characters.

Writing

Key writing purpose to be shared with the children:

To write a diary entry in role as Billy, exploring the final events of the story.

Writing evaluation to be shared with the children

My diary entry:

- explores how Billy's feelings change towards the dilemma
- uses interesting synonyms and adjectival phrases to build vivid descriptions
- builds suspense as Billy arrives at his final decision
- uses interesting comparisons to engage the reader in my descriptions.

Grammar:

- includes the first person and past tense to show the reader that I am writing in role as Billy
- includes a relative clause with 'which' 'or' 'where' to add information.

See the Planning section of the Software ('Timetables' tab) for a printable version of the Writing purpose and evaluation.

Fiction: A modern retelling of a myth/ dilemma story
Bling! by Jon Blake

READING FICTION

Resources

PB Pupils' Book, pp.15–25
A Anthology, pp.16–30
CD CD on interactive whiteboard, Unit 2
GB Grammar Bank on CD
HB Homework Book, pp.7–9

DAY 1

Curriculum link: identifying and discussing themes and conventions, making comparisons within and across books

The story store (CD)

Purpose: for children to understand what a dilemma is and to contextualise it within some well-known stories

- Write up and display the word 'dilemma' then contextualise it and clarify the meaning within some sentences, such as:

  If she played netball she would miss going to her best friend's party. Whatever she chose she would miss out and let people down. What a terrible dilemma.
- Look at the three story dilemmas on the **CD (file 1.1)**. Focus on the dilemmas for each of the characters but don't dwell on the choices they make in the end.
- Use TTYP (Turn to your partner) to explore the following three questions. Take examples of their ideas and collect some of them to return to later: *What is a dilemma? Why do stories have dilemmas? How can dilemmas be solved?*

read fiction

Read a story version 1 (CD)

Before the lesson, you may wish to watch the video demonstrating Read a story version 1 (with a Year 5 story). This can be found in the Extras section of the software.

Purpose: for children to become familiar with Story version 1; the bare bones of Bling!

- Read Story version1 aloud all the way through to the children. Do not read the numbers aloud. (Do not reveal the dilemma and the ending of the final story.)

  Story Version 1
  1. A lonely boy saved a magical being, which granted him a wish.
  2. The boy was given the power to turn things into gold.
  3. This power made the boy very popular.
  4. But the power had a downside. The boy became the target of other children, who wanted gold too.
  5. So the boy had to be protected all the time.
  6. One day the boy found the magic had left him with an awful dilemma.
  7. The magical being gave the boy a choice.
- Use MT/YT (My turn/Your turn), repeating each point – you will need to break down the longer points! Use exaggerated intonation and emphasis where appropriate to make the sentences memorable. This will help the children to 'hold' the basic story in their heads.
- Now display Story version 1 on the **CD (file 1.2)** for the children to read.

making comparisons, identifying themes

Think and link (CD)

Purpose: for children to make links and connections with other stories

- Return to the dilemmas in the Story store on the **CD (file 1.1)** and link them to Story version 1 by discussing the dilemmas that each character faces.
- Ask the children to TTYP and talk about where the dilemma is located in this story.
- Ask children to TTYP and discuss a dilemma they may have had, or ones they have heard of. Take feedback.

Curriculum link: predicting; identifying how language, structure, and presentation contribute to meaning

Read a story version 2 (CD)

Purpose: for children to examine how Story version 2 provides additional information for the reader and for children to become more familiar with the story before they hear the full version

- Read Story version 2 aloud to the children. Explain that it has been developed

Story version 2

1. Billy Midas was a lonely, unlucky boy who thought that he was a loser. His only loved possession was his beautiful cat Goji.
2. One day Billy rescued a tiny magical being called Chimichanga, who created a gold-maker for him; it would turn anything into gold.
3. Billy used his power to impress the cool kids at school. He changed their cheap jewellery into glowing gold and they became friends. Billy gleamed with satisfaction.
4. Soon other children learnt of Billy's power and they hurt him and stole some glittering gold from him.
5. Now Billy had to have bodyguards and protect himself all the time.
6. One awful day Billy returned home to find, to his horror, that he had a terrible dilemma.
7. Billy was distraught and frantically called for Chimichanga to help him.

- Re-read it, stopping after each section to ask the children if there are any words that tell them more about the people and the story TTYP and feedback.
- Now display this version on the **CD (file 1.3)**. Click 'Highlights' to identify how the story has changed. TOL (Think out loud) and use TTYP to share how this extra information changes the pictures in our minds as we hear the story.
- Hide the text and ask the children to use TTYP to take turns telling the story to each other taking one section at a time.

discuss their understanding of what they have read, predicting

Daily log – understanding a character (PB)

Purpose: for children to empathise with the main character

- Ask the children to TTYP and discuss the Understanding a character questions in the Pupils' Book p.15. Ask the children to make a prediction about how Billy's new power will make him feel and write it in their Daily log. Take feedback.

effective discussion; provide justifications for their views

Big Question (CD)

Purpose: for children to develop their skills of argument and discussion through a mini enquiry session based on a philosophical question relating to the work of the day

- Click on the 'Big Question' icon and display the day's Big Question on the **CD (file 1.4):**

Should we choose what is best for a few or for the majority?

- Ask the children to TTYP to discuss. Collect feedback from partners and scribe some responses. Tell the children that each day's Big Question and their thoughts will be collected on the CD and saved so that at the end of Week 2 they can then vote on which question to discuss more deeply. See Introduction for further notes (p.13).

DAY 2

discuss their understanding of what they have read

Read a story version 3 (A)

Purpose: for children to hear and enjoy the full version of the story for the first time

- Tell the children they are now going to hear the whole story for the very first time. TOL about which parts you are looking forward to.

Fiction: A modern retelling of a myth/ dilemma story

- Read aloud to the children the full story from the Anthology pp.16–25 with great enjoyment, and appropriate intonation. Make your storytelling a 'performance' and try to create tension for the delivery of the dilemma.
- Make sure the children understand the ending of the story. Read the final part of the story a second time and make sure the children realise that we are not told what Billy decides.
- Use TTYP to discuss the dilemma and how the children might solve it if they were in Billy's place. Take feedback.

Curriculum link: recognise themes in what they read, making comparisons

Context

Purpose: for children to link the story to the myth on which it is based

- Look at the summary of the King Midas myth on the **CD (File 2.1)**. Ask the children to TTYP to discuss anything they find similar about this story and the story you have been exploring. You may want to print the story map from **CD (file 2.2)**.
- Make links between the two characters showing how they have the same power. Ask the children to TTYP and discuss whether they think the power to turn things into gold is a good one and how it could cause problems. Take feedback.
- Click on the thought bubbles to reveal the thoughts which focus on the main points of similarity in the two stories. TOL how you show your own understanding of the story.

summarising the main ideas

Map the story

Purpose: for children to understand the chronology and main points of the story

- Display the story map of *Bling!* on the **CD (file 2.3)** and go through it using TOL to discuss what the main events are and what Billy's choices are as the story progresses. You may wish to reiterate the link between this story and the King Midas myth as you go along.

Curriculum link: summarising the main ideas, identifying key details

Daily log

Purpose: for children to create a written or drawn representation of the story that can be used as an aide-memoire

- Ask the children to map the story of *Bling!* in their Daily log. You may wish to display the version on the **CD (file 2.3)** as a scaffold. Encourage them to add in some extra details they found interesting from the story reading.

effective discussion; provide justifications for their views

Big Question

Purpose: for children to develop their skills of argument and discussion through a mini enquiry session based on a philosophical question relating to the work of the day

- Display today's Big Question on the **CD (file 2.4)**:

  What would you give up to have your greatest wish?

- Follow the process as explained at the end of Day 1 (p.47).

DAY 3

exploring the meaning of words in context

Word power

Purpose: for children to visualise strong descriptive phrases and think about how they help the reader engage with a story

glinted with the heavenly glow of gold *heavy with luxury* *glittering wrist*
glow of satisfaction *gleaming like gold* *gleaming with the terrible beauty*

- Explain to the children that you are going to look at some of the descriptive language used in the story. Display the Word power words on the **CD (file 3.1)**.
- Drag the phrases into the box and TOL describing the images these words bring to you as a reader. Make connections with the text as you link the phrases clearly with the images you are creating whilst reading. For example: *'In the text it says that "Billy's hand felt heavy with luxury"– that could mean that the gold felt heavier than the cheap metal but I think it also says something about how the gold felt luxurious, special and cool and made Billy feel luxurious.'*
- You may wish to print off the words from the **CD (file 3.2)** and display them on the Story wall.

explain and discuss their understanding of what they have read

Re-read a story version 3

Purpose: for children to gain a deeper understanding of the story and see the text for the first time

- Let the children see and follow their own copy of the text in the Anthology pp.16–25 as you re-read the full version of the story aloud to them with enthusiasm, enjoyment and appropriate intonation. Place special emphasis upon the Power words in bold.
- Now ask the children to read their copy of the story with their partners, reading alternate sections. Ask them to read together any words and phrases in bold with great expression. Explain that you will be listening in on readings.

Clarify

Purpose: for children to clarify their understanding of the story

- Use TOL to show your own understanding of the story. Read one section at a time, stopping after each section and thinking out loud to let the children 'see' your thought processes. Tell them that you are letting them see inside your mind as you read – as if you have a think bubble coming out of your head.

Don't make it look too easy. Hesitate and ask yourself questions and answer them yourself. Bring the children into the TOL. Ask them to locate the words and phrases you are talking about. Examples with text and think bubbles pre-selected can be found on the **CD (file 3.3)**.

Curriculum link: Year 5 Grammar
relative clauses with 'where' and 'which'

Grammar: relative clauses 1 CD PB HB

Purpose: for children to recognise relative clauses and understand their function in adding more detail to a noun

- Remind the children that there are lots of different types of sentences and ask them if they can remember what a complex sentence is. Take feedback and, if necessary, remind the children that complex sentences are made up of two clauses: a main clause that makes sense on its own and a less important (subordinate) clause that doesn't make sense on its own, but adds more information to the main clause.
- Display the **CD (file 3.4)** and use MT/YT to read out the sentence. Say that this is a complex sentence with two clauses. Click 'Highlights' to show the two clauses highlighted in different colours. Ask the children to TTYP and decide which is the subordinate clause (if necessary, remind them that a subordinate clause does not make sense on its own).
- Take feedback, confirming that 'where he normally stored the cushion' is the subordinate clause. Ensure children understand that 'Billy's eyes immediately went to the top of the wardrobe' is the main clause because it makes sense on its own.
- Click to the next slide and repeat with the second sentence, asking the children to identify the subordinate clause.
- Say that both subordinate clauses that you have looked at started with the same word. Ask the children to TTYP to decide which word this is, then ask them to give feedback chorally. (They should identify the word 'where'.)
- Explain that this word is important because it tells us what sort of subordinate clause it is. The word 'where' tells us that this is the start of a relative clause, which is a type of subordinate clause.
- Tell the children that another word that can start a relative clause is 'which'. Click to the next slide to display the sentence. Use MT/YT to read out the sentence, then ask the children to TTYP and decide which is the relative clause. Take feedback, then click 'Highlights' to show the two clauses and TOL bubbles. TOL as you read the notes.
- Click to the next slide and do the same for the next sentence, using the term 'relative clause' as much as possible and encourage the children to use it too.
- Warn the children that the words 'which' or 'where' can also be used at the start of a question. They only introduce relative clauses if they are part of a longer, complex sentence.
- Ask the children to look at the Grammar: relative clauses 1 activity on p.15 of their Pupils' Book. Tell them to TTYP to complete the activity orally. Ask them to feed back their answers, while you clarify where necessary.

Homework Book p.7 provides further practice on relative clauses.

exploring the meaning of words in context

Daily log – Images PB

Purpose: for children to contextualise and discuss descriptive language they have explored in the text

- Tell the children to TTYP to do the Images activity in the Pupils' Book p.16.

Model scanning skills so that the children can locate the phrases and then zoom in on the words, looking at their context and discussing the images that they bring up for them.

- Ask them to write a couple of their favourite phrases in their Daily log.

Curriculum link: effective discussion; provide justifications for their views

Big Question (CD)

Purpose: for children to develop their skills of argument and discussion through a mini enquiry session based on a philosophical question relating to the work of the day

- Display today's Big Question on the **CD (file 3.5)**:

Which is more important possessions or people?

- Follow the process as explained at the end of Day 1 (p.47).

DAY 4

checking that the story makes sense to them

Re-read a story version 3 (CD)

Purpose: for children to understand how the author gives clues in the text about how a character is feeling

- Read the three short excerpts from the story on the **CD (file 4.1)** aloud to the children to find out more about Billy at school. Read each extract in turn, highlighting how Billy is moving and how he talks to other children.
- Discuss how Billy's attitude to his new friends seems to be changing by the third passage.
- Use TTYP to reflect upon how Billy has changed since gaining his power. Make sure you show where in the text you are finding the clues that show how Billy changes and if possible model using inference or deduction through TOL.

For example: 'Billy doesn't seem to be as interested in Goji any more, perhaps he doesn't need her as much. It says here he only gave her a "brief tickle, then got down to the important business". I can infer from this that making gold is more important than playing with Goji and that's a real change in Billy.

exploring the meaning of words in context

Special phrases (CD) (print)

Purpose: for children to explore the imagery in the story

Goji was his cat, a lean fishbone tabby so perfectly marked she was a natural miracle.

The next day, Billy strolled into school as cool as a cucumber.

A glow of satisfaction spread through Billy, until he was sure his whole being must be gleaming like gold.

He walked with a slow swagger and a poker face, because top dogs didn't need to smile.

- Before starting this activity share the terms 'metaphor' and 'simile' with the class and check they understand their meaning.
- Display some of the sentences from the story on the **CD (file 4.2)**. Click 'TOL' to reveal the think bubbles, which explore some of the imagery – similes and metaphors – in the story.
- Encourage the children to choose one or two of the phrases to add to their Daily log.
- You may wish to print out some of the sentences from the **CD (file 4.3)** as model sentences for your Story wall.

discuss and evaluate how authors use language

Word play (CD)

Purpose: for children to explore synonyms for 'walked'

- Focus the children on the moment when Billy first crosses the playground to show off his bling to Calum and Ed on the **CD (file 4.4)**.

- Ask them to put themselves in Billy's shoes and visualise that walk. TOL: '*The story says Billy swaggers but I don't think he always walked that way.*'
- Display the Word play words on the **CD (file 4.5)**.
- Work together using TOL and TTYP to decide how a character might walk depending on his status. Explain when Billy was a worm he might not want to be noticed so he might creep. Drag "creep" into the "worm" box.
- Repeat the process, giving partners time to decide where each word should go and taking feedback.

Curriculum link: discuss viewpoints

Drama – status game

Purpose: for children to see that your status can be shown by the way you move

- Organise the children to work in small groups (no more than five per group).
- Give all the children except one the status cards numbered on a scale of 1–4 (ensuring roles are given out sensitively). Tell them 4 is "top dog" and 1 is "playground worm". The child without the card is the observer.
- Ask them to move around in a small space in role showing their status by their movements.
- Tell them to watch the other members of their group. When they come close to other group members children should defer to those they think are higher status and be imposing to those they think are lower status.
- At the end of a few minutes of role-play ask the observer to get the children in status order.
- Ask the children to reveal the 'true' order.
- Ask the children to TTYP to discuss which physical clues denoted different statuses. Take feedback.

discussing their understanding and exploring the meaning of words in context

Daily log – synonyms PB

Purpose: for children to link the way a character moves to how they are feeling

- Ask the children to TTYP to do the Synonyms activity in the Pupils' Book p.16 using their ideas from the Drama status game and the work about how Billy has changed. Children can then add the synonyms for 'walk' to their Daily log.

effective discussion; provide justifications for their views

Big Question CD

Purpose: for children to develop their skills of argument and discussion through a mini enquiry session based on a philosophical question relating to the work of the day

- Display today's Big Question on the **CD (file 4.6)**:

  Is the truth easy to see?*

- Follow the process as explained at the end of Day 1 (p.47).

* *This Big Question will be revisited on Day 11 – the first day of the Non-fiction week.*

DAY 5

checking that the story makes sense to them, discussing their understanding

Consequences A

Purpose: for children to understand that actions have consequences and that these take the plot forward

- Ask the children to TTYP to recap on how Billy's feelings have changed over the story.
- Read out the section where Billy gets robbed on his way home. Put real emphasis on how Billy speaks. Make him sound serious and a bit mean.

- Use TOL to discuss how Billy's life has changed. For example:

  'Before he was unimportant at school and now he is important, but he has to be protected.'

  'Before he felt he was a loser and now he hangs out with the coolest boys, but he has started to despise them.'
- Now ask the children to take turns to read the section of the story to each other from when Billy returns home to find an eerie silence, in the Anthology p.23.
- Tell the children that actions have consequences. For example, if you spill your drink the consequence is that you might get wet and you could be thirsty. We cannot always predict what the consequences of our actions will be. Just like Billy we could do something small that could end up having a large consequence.
- Ask the children to find out what actions led to the consequence of Goji turning to gold. (Billy hadn't locked his bedroom door and he'd left the cushion on his desk.)
- Take feedback from the pairs and point out exactly where in the text the information is found.

Curriculum link: drawing inferences and justifying with evidence, identifying key details that support ideas

What if not...? PB

Purpose: for children to consider the impact of changes made to a text

- Ask the children to look at the What if not...? questions in the Pupils' Book p.17. Model how you consider the first What if not...? What if not a *'loser'*? What if Billy had been *popular*?
- Ask children to TTYP and discuss this and the other What if not...? questions. Collect feedback and encourage others to build an argument. Give your opinion too.

noting ideas

Daily log

Purpose: for children to chart how Billy has changed through the story

- Ask the children to continue thinking about Billy before and after the gold-maker and write another two examples of how Billy has changed in their Daily log.

consider different accounts of the same event and discuss viewpoints

Drama – hotseating CD PB

Purpose: for the children to understand Billy's dilemma from his point of view

- Ask the children to TTYP and discuss the Hotseating – warm up questions in the Pupils' Book p.17. Take feedback.
- Tell the children you are going to act as Billy finding Goji petrified in gold. Then you are going to stay in role as you are asked questions. Tell the children that they need to keep notes in their Daily log to return to later when they are writing.
- Give another adult or the children the pre-prepared questions from the **CD (file 5.1)**. This list is not exhaustive and you may wish to adapt or add to them.
- After the hotseating use TTYP to discuss what the children think Billy should do at the end of the story.
- Take feedback on the pros and cons of his possible actions and list on the interactive whiteboard, see **CD (file 5.2)**.

Curriculum link: effective discussion; provide justifications for their views

Big Question

Purpose: for children to develop their skills of argument and discussion through a mini enquiry session based on a philosophical question relating to the work of the day

- Display today's Big Question on the **CD (file 5.3)**:

  Is power everything?

- Follow the process as explained at the end of Day 1 (p.47).

WRITING FICTION

DAY 6

pupils should understand, through being shown, the skills and processes essential for writing: thinking aloud to generate ideas, drafting, and re-reading to check that the meaning is clear

Build a sentence

Purpose: for children to create a vivid image using description and comparison

- Reveal the sentence describing Goji on the **CD (file 6.1)**. Read it aloud and comment on how the author has listed attributes of the living Goji and compared them to the gold dead statue. Explain to the children how the comparison gives us a strong image of how Goji has changed.
- Click on sentence 1, **CD (file 6.2)** to reveal the choices of words that could be used to describe Goji as a statue contrasted to Goji alive. Re-read the sentence using substitutions to describe the cat. The sentences have been adapted slightly from the Anthology text for the purpose of the activity.
- Ask the children to TTYP to comment on the effect of different word combinations. Take feedback about the different descriptions.
- Repeat for sentence 2 generating descriptions of Goji the statue in contrast with Goji the living cat.
- Ask the children to TTYP their own preferred version of the sentence. Take feedback.

Modelled composition

- Now use modelled composition to write the first two sentences of a new story.
- A script of the writing process can be printed from the **CD (file 6.3)** if you want more support.Modelled composition text:

  Billy gazed at Goji who was now a cold, golden statue and imagined how it would be to hold her warm, purring body again. He remembered her calm, comforting presence, which he missed desperately, and the way she used to be his most prized friend.

- Use TOL to explain what you are doing and orally rehearse and change each phrase before you write. Focus on the words you choose to compare Goji alive and when Goji has been turned to gold. Explain why you are bringing back the memory of her alive in the second sentence to show Billy's feelings for her.
- Ask the children to say each sentence as you compose it using MT/YT and then write it on a flipchart or the board. Continue to use these prompts as you now TOL and model the writing process.
- Now hide your sentences. Ask the children, either individually or as partners, to compose their own sentence out loud using the prompts in the Build a sentence activity in the Pupils' Book p.18. Once the children can say the sentence out loud, they should write it in their Daily log.
- Ask partners to take turns to develop each other's sentences. Encourage crossings out, switching words round, etc. Emphasise that this is writing in action – it is not a neat, finished piece of writing!

Curriculum link: making comparisons

Tell a story

Purpose: for children to develop their awareness of the differences between oral and written stories; for children to develop confidence in building a story orally

- Show the short text on the **CD (file 6.4)** that builds on the sentences from the last activity. This text builds Billy's dilemma.

  Billy gazed at Goji who was now a cold, golden statue and imagined how it would be to hold her warm, purring body again. He remembered her calm, comforting presence which he missed desperately, and the way she used to be his most prized friend.

- Explain that you are going to have a go at retelling this part of the story to them without looking at the written text (prepare your oral retelling before the lesson). They will need to remember your retelling as much as possible so that they can then compare it to the written version in the Pupils' Book. Ask them to listen carefully for:
  - missing information
  - additional information
  - how the order of the story might be different
  - more everyday language and less description
  - use of body language, facial expressions to emphasise and engage the audience, etc.
- After the oral retelling ask the children to TTYP to share what differences they noticed. They can refer to the full written version of the text in the Pupils' Book p.18 whilst discussing the retelling. Collect feedback.
- Tell the children that they are going re-read the story so far in the Tell a story activity in the Pupils' Book and then continue and develop the story orally with their partners. They should swap roles from teller to listener and vice versa when you say *stop and swap* at about 30 second intervals (two or three times), continuing the story from that point each time. Emphasis should be on building confidence in storytelling and keeping their audience engaged and interested!

noting initial ideas

Daily log

Purpose: for children to start to generate and record ideas for their story

- Ask the children to write down one of the ideas they discussed with their partner for continuing the story in their Daily log.

effective discussion; provide justifications for their views

Big Question

Purpose: for children to develop their skills of argument and discussion through a mini enquiry session based on a philosophical question relating to the work of the day

- Display today's Big Question on the **CD (file 6.5)**:

  Are we responsible for the consequences of our actions – even if they are unintentional?

- Follow the process as explained at the end of Day 1 (p.47).

DAY 7

considering how authors have developed characters

Build a character

Purpose: for children to understand the main character's motivation to predict how they might act

- Explain to the children that a vital ingredient of a successful dilemma story is the character. As readers we have to feel that we really understand the character so that we care about their problems. As writers we must be able to make our character interesting, sympathetic and their dilemma a struggle that the reader could identify with.

- Display the image and description of Billy on the **CD (file 7.1)**.
- Read a fact about Billy and use TOL to show the children where in the text this fact comes from and then use this information to make a judgement about Billy's character, for example:
  TOL: '*It says Billy thinks he's a loser – in the story the narrator says this right from the start, Billy doesn't have the right trainers, it says at school he is unimportant – a "worm". I would say Billy isn't very confident.*'
- Ask the children to TTYP and discuss the other facts about Billy and come to a conclusion about what they say about Billy's character. Take feedback and write the main ideas in a list.
- Draw the children's attention to the fact that the narrator doesn't *say* that Billy isn't confident, that he is lonely or that he is kind but he *shows* them through his actions.
- Ask the children to TTYP and discuss how they think Billy's character will act faced with his dilemma. Collect feedback.

Curriculum link: developing initial ideas

Daily log

Purpose: for children to keep a personal reading, writing and thinking log to record thoughts and ideas for their own writing

- Ask the children to collect some of their ideas about how they think Billy will solve his dilemma in their Daily log.

learn the conventions of different types of writing, such as the use of the first person in writing diaries

Build a story ending 1 A CD

Purpose: for children to see how to plan a diary entry using the story text for information

- Now that the children have explored Billy's character a bit further they are more able to see the story through his eyes. Explain that you are going to model the planning and writing of a diary entry that retells the beginning of the story from Billy's point of view.
- Ask the children to turn to the story in the Anthology p.16 and read the first part where Billy finds Chimichanga and is given the gold-maker.
- When they have refreshed their memories about this episode say that you are going to use a 'helping hand' that asks five key questions to organise your ideas.
- Use TTYP throughout this activity after you display each question so that the children can discuss what information they can find in the text.
- Now display the helping hand on the **CD (file 7.2)** and click on each of the words to reveal the questions. Say the answers are from Billy as he is going to be writing the diary entry. TTYP: What could Billy's answer be? Then click on the words again to reveal the planning sentences.

plan their writing by using similar writing as models for their own

Build a story ending 2 CD PB

Purpose: for children to see an example of the text they will be writing

- Read aloud to the children Billy's diary entry on the **CD (file 7.4)** and talk through the key features (first person; past tense; chronological order; adverbs and adverbials of time, such as *next, after that,* etc; personal responses) highlighting them as you go.
- Print off a copy of the diary entry for each of the partners from the **CD (file 7.3)**. Using TTYP and oral feedback, ask the children to evaluate 'your' writing using the Build a story ending 2 guide questions in the Pupils' Book p.19.

7.3 - Diary entry.
- make notes of vocab.
8.1 - Bare bones of the diary entry.

Curriculum link: evaluate how authors use language

Daily log

Purpose: for children to re-read the r… for their own writing

- Ask the children to take turns … from the **CD (file 7.3)**, highligh… …uage that they might like to borrow … vocabulary they like best in their…

effective discussion; provide justifications for their views

Big Question

Purpose: for children to develop their sk… enquiry session based on a ph… …ating to the work of the day

- Display today's Big Question on the **CD (file 7.5)**:

  What would you give up for love?

- Follow the process as explained at the end of Day 1 (p.47).

DAY 8

drawing inferences and justifying these with evidence, predicting

Dilemma drama

Purpose: for children to explore Billy's dilemma and the consequences of the choice he takes

- Tell the children that they are going to write a diary entry in role as Billy. This is going to cover the final events of the story. Ask them to read the final section of the story in the Anthology p.24 from when Billy calls for Chimichanga to help him, to remind them of the dilemma he has to face.
- Ask the children to TTYP and turn to the Dilemma drama activity in the Pupils' Book p.20. Ask them to use the prompts to help work out the reasons for and consequences of Billy keeping the gold-maker, and those of him giving it up and all the gold returning to its original state. Move around the room noting good ideas and arguments. Give feedback.

plan their writing using similar writing as models for their own

Write a story 1

Purpose: for children to plan a diary entry

- Read aloud to the children the bare bones of the dilemma diary entry on the **CD (file 8.1)**.
- Ask the children to use the information they have gathered from the dilemma drama to compose the bare bones for their diary entry in their Daily log.

write by selecting appropriate grammar and vocabulary

Write a story 2

Purpose: for children to develop sentences and description in their diary entry

- Using TOL, and encouraging the children to offer their ideas, model how to develop sentence 1 by adding some information and phrases, and changing some words.
- Repeat using sentence 2.
- Ask the children to do the Write a story 2 activity in the Pupils' Book p.21 and to develop sentence 3 on the **CD (file 8.1)** using the prompts. Explain that you want them to compose individually their sentence in their heads first. They must then make sure they can say their opening sentence to their partner before they start to write.
- Now display this developed version of sentence 4 on the **CD (file 8.2)**:

  The Chimichanga stared into my eyes as if it were searching my soul. It looked from me to Goji and sighed before explaining that if I wanted Goji to return to life I'd have to give up the gold-maker and accept that everything turned to gold would return back to its former state.

- Guide children to identify features that show the development.
- Ask the children to develop sentence 5 from the **CD (file 8.1).** Again explain that you want them to compose individually their sentence in their heads first. They must then make sure they can say their opening sentence to their partner before they start to write.

Curriculum link: consider different accounts of the same event

Daily log

Purpose: for children to consider the dilemma from another point of view

- Ask the children to write in role as Calum, the cool child at school, and give Billy a piece of advice about what he should do.

effective discussion; provide justifications for their views

Big Question (CD)

Purpose: for children to develop their skills of argument and discussion through a mini enquiry session based on a philosophical question relating to the work of the day

- Display today's Big Question on the **CD (file 8.3)**:

  What is popularity?

- Follow the process as explained at the end of Day 1 (p.47).

DAY 9

draft and write by describing settings, characters and atmosphere

Write a story 3 PB (CD)

Purpose: for children to write a diary entry for Billy's point of view that concludes the story

- Tell the children that they are ready to write their own final diary entry from Billy's point of view explaining what he decides to do about his dilemma and the possible consequences of his decision. Ask them to use the Write a story 3 composition prompts in the Pupils' Book p.22. Remind them to use any useful parts of their Daily log to help them.
- Point out that they can add more information to sentences by adding a relative clause with 'which' or 'where' as they were shown on Day 3.
- Remind them to look at the Story wall for Power words and phrases and a thesaurus for synonyms.
- Encourage children to rehearse their opening sentence with their partners before they begin to write.
- You may wish to display the paper showing the sentences you modelled with the children and/or the developed sentence 4 on the **CD (file 9.1)**.

DAY 10

assessing the effectiveness of their own and others' writing

Share a story

Purpose: for children to read and share their diary entry

- Ask the children to read through their own diary entry from Day 9.
- Now tell them to re-read their diary entry and underline their favourite or best parts. Ask them to share these with their partners. Collect feedback on best bits from partners.
- Make sure that any powerful words or phrases are written on card and added to the Story wall.

Evaluate and edit (CD)

Purpose: for children to evaluate their own and their partner's work against specific criteria and then discuss how they could improve their work

- Display **CD (file 10.1)** to show the evaluation prompts and read them together using MT/YT.
- As a model, select an example of work from the children where the writing has met the criteria, and share this with the other children, explaining why it works well.
- Tell the children to take turns to read their partner's writing and discuss how well they have met the criteria.
- Ask children to discuss at least two changes they could make to improve their work following the partner discussion.

Curriculum link: proof-read for spelling and punctuation errors

Proofread

Purpose: for children to proofread their work and make changes to improve the accuracy of their grammar, punctuation and spelling

- Now ask the children to proofread their work. If you have noticed that several children need to improve on a particular aspect of spelling, grammar or punctuation, use this as a focus for the Proofread activity. Write an example which includes common errors from the children's writing and use this as a model.
- The children should always be checking for standard use of punctuation and correct spelling of common exception words.
- The following points would be relevant as the particular focus for this Unit:
  - checking for consistent use of the first person and past tense
  - checking for correct use of relative clauses with 'where' or 'which'
  - checking spelling of more ambitious vocabulary choices.

effective discussion; provide justifications for their views, distinguish between fact and opinion

Very Big Question (CD)

Purpose: for children to develop their willingness to broaden or revise their opinions through exploring one of the Big Questions in more depth

- See Unit 1 Day 10 for teaching notes on the Very Big Question (p.36).

Recounts

READING AND WRITING NON-FICTION

The non-fiction part of this Unit links to the fiction through exploring the difference between a first person recount, such as a diary, and a newspaper report of the same event. Children compose their own newspaper report for a younger audience, based on a real-life rescue and adapt it for the radio.

See p.44 for the daily timetable for the Non-fiction week.

Non-fiction

Reading

Children will:

- learn how a reporter's description of an event might not always be reliable
- learn how pejorative language can show the reader the point of view from which a newspaper recount is written
- identify the key features of a newspaper article and discuss how these make a recount easier to follow.

Writing

Key writing purpose to be shared with the children:

To write a newspaper recount that is suitable for a younger reader.

Writing evaluation to be shared with the children

My newspaper recount:

- is easy to follow because I have used organisational features of newspapers, e.g. *headline, subheading, captions* and *pictures*
- has details about the event and quotes from eye-witness accounts, to engage the reader's interest
- ensures the reader feels informed of all the key facts
- is written in an informal style for younger readers.

Grammar:

- includes relative clauses to provide extra information for the reader.

See the Planning section of the Software ('Timetables' tab) for a printable version of the Writing purpose and evaluation.

DAY 11

Curriculum link: consider different accounts of the same event and discuss viewpoints

Linking the texts

Purpose: for children to make links between the story text and the non-fiction text

- Display the Big Question from Day 4 on the **CD (file 4.6)**: *Is the truth easy to see?*
- Review the ideas the children had about this question and then draw their attention to the fact that often we cannot see all aspects of the truth.
- Make a link between how an event is reported and the reporter's point of view, by explaining that a reporter works with the evidence that they can gather which could mean they do not have the whole picture.
- Watch *The Guardian* advert about point of view on the **CD (file 11.1)** which clearly shows how point of view can affect a person's understanding of an event.
- Ask the children to TTYP and discuss what they have seen. Collect feedback.

learn the conventions of different types of writing

Introduction

Purpose: for children to understand the context for the study of the non-fiction recount text

- Recap on the story *Bling!* and discuss how Billy's amazing powers could well have caught the attention of teachers and parents. What might happen if a newspaper heard about the extraordinary goings-on at Billy's school? Explain that often newspapers like to have 'an angle' – they don't just want to give the facts of the story but also highlight one aspect of it such as the threat to Billy from bigger kids now that he wears so much gold.
- Ask the children to TTYP and discuss what angle a reporter might take on Billy's story. Take feedback.
- Explain that you and another adult are going to act in role as a reporter and Calum (the cool boy from the story). Set up an interview situation with questions that lead Calum into talking about the trouble the gold has brought. See **CD (file 11.2)** for an example script for you to use if you need more support.
- Ask the children to TTYP and discuss the angle that the reporter had. Ask the children to try to identify any particular leading questions. Can they explain how the questions might influence Calum's reply?

discuss viewpoints, exploring the meaning of words in context

Points of view

Purpose: for children to explore the point of view an article is written from

- Explain that the interview has now been put into an article about the phenomenon.
- Explain that this recount has a definite angle and that this is highlighted through the use of pejorative language (words that show the writer has made a negative judgement e.g. troubled parents).
- Ask the children to take turns reading aloud a section of the article in the Points of view activity in the Pupils' Book p.23. Ask them to TTYP and discuss which of the words or phrases give away the reporter's point of view that Billy should be worried about his safety. Tell them to write the most powerful pejorative words or phrases in their Daily log. Discuss the perjorative words e.g. fearing, gangs of youths, easy pickings.

Zoom in on recounts

Purpose: for children to become familiar with some words and synonyms associated with recount texts

chronological order *adverbs and adverbials of time* *orientation* *formal/formality*

- Display the words and their definitions on the **CD (file 11.3)**. Look at them with the children and read each sentence. Ask them to repeat the sentences using MT/YT.
- Print off the words and their definitions from the **CD (file 11.4)**. Display the words on your Non-fiction wall. The children must hear, see and repeat the word in your teaching and conversation throughout the day.
- Now tell the children to do the Zoom in on recounts activity in the Pupils' Book p.24.

Curriculum link: noting initial ideas, drawing on reading and research

Daily log

Purpose: for children to keep a personal reading, writing and thinking log to record thoughts and ideas for their own writing

- Tell the children that over the next few days, you want them to look in magazines, in newspapers, and on the Internet, for recounts of actual events. Ask them to cut them out or save them (asking permission first) and bring them to school to stick them in their Daily log. Tell them to write a note next to each one of where they found it. Tell them to make sure they are not all from the Internet!

DAY 12

plan their writing by using other similar writing as models for their own

Deconstruction 1

Purpose: for children to see an example of writing that will provide a model for the planning of their own writing

- Ask the children to find the 'Bravery Award for Fire Hero Boy' text in the Anthology pp.26–27. Tell them to follow the text as you read it aloud with lots of expression, enthusiasm and appropriate intonation.
- Now display the text on the **CD (file 12.1)** and draw the children to the key features of a newspaper recount by highlighting: picture, captions, headlines, formal tone, quotations, past tense and details including place names and names and ages of people.
- Explain to the children that this text will be used as a reference to help them to plan their own recount for a younger audience. Ask them to read their copy of the Anthology text with their partners, reading alternate sections each. Ask them to TTYP to share whether the recount says clearly:
  - who the recount is about
  - where and when it happened
  - what happened
  - why the event took place.
- Ask: 'Is there too much extra information or details, or is it just right?'

retrieve information

Read a recount

Purpose: for children to understand and locate examples of the key features of a recount text

- Display the Key features checklist grid on the **CD (file 12.3)**. Explain the completed examples in the grid: 'Adverbs and adverbials of time' and 'Different viewpoints'.
- Tell the children to work with their partners to complete their own grids. They can be printed from the **CD (file 12.2)** for children to record their answers.
- Collect answers and complete the grid on the CD to clarify points and show different examples.

DAY 13

Curriculum link:
identifying the audience

Deconstruction 2 CD PB

Purpose: for children to explore how complex sentences and use of detailed information can convey a formal tone

- Display the extracts from the 'Bravery Award for Fire Hero Boy' text on the **CD (file 13.1)** and highlight pieces of the text that show the degree of formality. Use TOL to comment on how and why this is done. The colour coding shows the sentences deconstucted. (Black shows the main clauses.)
- Ask the children to TTYP and discuss why this style might be inappropriate for a younger audience. Take feedback.
- Ask the children to look at the Deconstruction 2 activity in the Pupils' Book p.25. They should take turns reading aloud a section of the article adapted for a younger audience. Ask them to TTYP and discuss in which ways it is different to the more formal newspaper article (e.g. clear link between the opening sentence and the headline; less formal; shorter; less detail; simpler sentences).

Year 5
Grammar
relative clauses beginning with 'who' and 'whose'

Grammar: relative clauses 2 CD PB HB

Purpose: for children to recognise relative clauses and understand their function in adding more detail to a noun

- Remind the children that earlier in the unit they looked at relative clauses which started with the words 'where' and 'which' (Day 3). Write the following sentence on the board *The fire fighter looked at the old oven where the fire had started.* Ask the children to TTYP and decide which is the main clause and which is the relative clause. (If they need a prompt, remind them that the main clause makes sense on its own, but the relative clause doesn't.) Take feedback checking their understanding of main and relative clauses.
- Display the **CD (file 13.2)**. Use MT/YT to read the sentence. Explain that this complex sentence has a relative clause, but this time it is introduced by the word 'who' rather than 'where' or 'which'.
- Ask the children to TTYP and decide which part of the sentence is the relative clause. Take feedback and then click 'Highlight' to show the relative clause and TOL bubble.
- Click to the next slide and repeat with the second sentence, explaining that this time the word, whose, is used to introduce the relative clause. Click 'Highlights' to show the relative clause and a TOL bubble. TOL about how this relative clause is slotted in between two parts of the main clause. Ensure the children understand that the main clause is 'Connor's father Shaun…was also at the scene in Green Lane', but the relative clause is like a sandwich filling – in the middle of two parts.
- Tell the children that relative clauses are often found in recounts such as newspaper articles, because they help to give extra information without using too many words or extra sentences.
- Ask the children to look at the Grammar: relative clauses 2 activity on p.25 of their Pupils' Book. Tell them to TTYP to complete the activity orally. Ask them to feed back their answers clarifying where necessary.
- Point out to the children that sometimes the words *who*, *that* or *which* are omitted from a relative clause, particularly in speech. Give some examples, e.g. *There's the thief I saw stealing the money. That was a weekend we all enjoyed.* Ask children to TTYP and say a similar sentence of their own. Take feedback and clarify where necessary.

Homework Book p.9 provides further practice on relative clauses.

Curriculum link: plan their writing by identifying the audience for and purpose of the writing

Build a recount

Purpose: for children to develop their confidence and skills in planning a recount text

- Tell the children that they are going to develop a plan for a recount about the teenage hero Conor McGrath for a younger pupil in Year 3. They will need to think about how to simplify the article for their audience, for example by using fewer quotations and more subheadings. Display the Recount planning grid on the **CD (file 13.4)**.
- Ask the children to use the 'Bravery Award for Fire Hero Boy' text in the Anthology to help them to fill in the details of the rescue in their planning grid. This can be printed from the **CD (file 13.3)** for children to write on.
- Walk around as they are working, noting good examples to add to the CD grid during the feedback session. Allow time for partners to share their ideas before asking for feedback.

discuss and evaluate how authors use language

Daily log

Purpose: for children to keep a personal reading, writing and thinking log to record thoughts and ideas for their own writing

- Tell the children that there are some very helpful quotes in the 'Bravery Award for Fire Hero Boy' newspaper article that give exciting detail about the amazing rescue. Ask them to choose their favourite quotation and copy it in their Daily log. Then ask them to add a couple of sentences explaining what they like about it.

DAY 14

assessing the effectiveness of others' writing

Deconstruction 3 – evaluate layout

Purpose: for children to see an example of writing that will provide an opportunity for them to evaluate the effectiveness of layout, organisation and clarity

- Tell the children that one of the most common forms of a non-fiction recount is a news report. Ask them to find the short reports from a newspaper and the Internet in the Anthology pp.28–30 and to follow the text as you read them out loud with lots of expression, enthusiasm and appropriate intonation.
- Now ask the children to take turns to read them to each other one section at a time. Explain that:
  - The writer of the Newshound report had a younger audience in mind and therefore had to use language that was easy to follow and had a less formal tone.
  - The writer used images and captions to make it easy for the reader to find extra information.
  - He chose to help the reader by using a headline that tells the reader what the news story is about and subheadings to help the reader know what is coming next. We call this the 'layout' and 'organisation' of the information on the page.
- Ask the children to TTYP and discuss how the different recounts are displayed. Ask them to use the features checklist from Day 12 on the **CD (file 12.2)** to see how effective these recounts are.
- Collect feedback.

writing non-fiction

Write a recount

Purpose: for children to use their planning grid to help them to write a full length recount text

- Display the example of a completed planning grid on the **CD (file 14.1)**.
- Explain that you are going to show how the plan can be used to create a recount text. Click on the **CD (file 14.2)** to display the recount and TOL using the think bubbles to help you.

- Tell the children that they are ready to write their rescue story recount using their planning grids.

  Remind them to:
  - use the features checklist from Day 12 to help them
  - use any useful parts of their Daily log
  - look at the example texts in the Anthology pp.28–30 ('Newshound' and 'Beach Bonanza!') and the adapted article in the Pupils' Book p.25
  - lInclude a relative clauses to add more information to a sentence.
  - use a thesaurus for synonyms.
- Encourage the children to rehearse their opening sentence with their partners before they begin to write.

Curriculum link: provide reasoned justifications for their views

Daily log

Purpose: for children to keep a personal reading, writing and thinking log to record thoughts and ideas for their own writing

- Ask the children to write three reasons why Conor should be awarded a bravery award. They may wish to rank them in order of importance.

DAY 15

assessing the effectiveness of their own and others' writing

Evaluate and edit (CD)

Purpose: for children to evaluate their own and their partner's work against specific criteria and then discuss how they could improve their work

- Display **CD (file 15.1)** to show the evaluation prompts and read them together using MT/YT.
- As a model, select an example of work from the children where the writing has met the criteria, and share this with the other children, explaining why it works well.
- Tell the children to take turns to read their partner's writing and discuss how well they have met the criteria.
- Ask children to discuss at least two changes they could make to improve their work following the partner discussion.

proofread for spelling and punctuation errors

Proofread

Purpose: for children to proofread their work and make changes to improve the accuracy of their grammar, punctuation and spelling

- Now ask the children to proofread their work. If you have noticed that several children need to improve on a particular aspect of spelling, grammar or punctuation, use this as a focus for the Proofread activity. Write an example which includes common errors from the children's writing and use this as a model.
- The children should always be checking for standard use of punctuation and correct spelling of common exception words.
- The following points would be relevant as the particular focus for this Unit:
  - checking use of capital letters for proper nouns
  - checking for correct use of relative clauses with 'who' or 'whose'
  - checking quotations are correctly punctuated.

Fiction: Poetic style
Non-fiction: Persuasive writing

Timetable

WEEK 1 Reading fiction *Poetry*

Day 1	Day 2	Day 3	Day 4	Day 5
The poetry store	Word power 1	Word power 2	Re-read the poem	Who says?
Introducing the poem 1	Think and link 2	Special phrases	Personification 1	Dramatic reconstruction
Introducing the poem 2	Introducing the poem 3	Read the poem	Personification 2	Daily log
Think and link 1	Daily log	Daily log	Daily log	Big Question
Daily log	Big Question	Big Question	Big Question	
Big Question				

WEEK 2 Writing fiction *Poetry*

Day 6	Day 7	Day 8	Day 9	Day 10
What if not...?	Build a poem 1	Write a poem 1	Write a poem 3	Share a poem
Build an image	Build a poem 2	Write a poem 2		Evaluate and edit
Daily log	Build a poem 3	Daily log		Proofread
Big Question	Daily log	Big Question		Very Big Question
	Big Question			

WEEK 3 Reading and writing non-fiction Persuasive writing

Day 11	Day 12	Day 13	Day 14	Day 15
Introduction	Deconstruction 1	Deconstruction 2	Deconstruction 3	Persuasive presentations
Word power	Grammar: adverbs of possibility	Persuasive language	Write a persuasive text 3	Evaluate and edit
Persuasive texts	Write a persuasive text 1	Grammar: modal verbs	Daily log	Daily log
Audience and purpose	Daily log	Write a persuasive text 2		
Daily log		Proofread		
		Daily log		

: shows that a file should be printed out from the Software.

Overview of the Unit

The children will study the poems 'Goodnight Stroud' by Pie Corbett and 'Last Night, I Saw the City Breathing' by Andrew Fusek Peters which have been chosen for their similar themes, strong imagery, rich vocabulary and use of powerful personification. The outcome of the poetry section of the Unit will be for the children to compose a free verse poem.

The Non-fiction part of the Unit is linked to the 'cities' theme of the poetry and explores persuasive writing. For more information about the Non-fiction week and the Non-fiction writing evaluation criteria, see p.81.

The Homework Book provides a homework activity related to the content of this Unit for each of the three weeks.

Poetry

Reading

Children will:

- read a range of poems about the city and make connections with their own experiences and other poems they have read
- explore how poets use language for effect
- consolidate their understanding of poetic terms, e.g. *rhyme, rhythm, alliteration, simile, metaphor* and *personification*
- perform a poem using expression to show understanding.

Writing

Key writing purpose to be shared with the children:

To write a poem about a classroom, building vivid images in my reader's mind.

Writing evaluation to be shared with the children

My poem:

- uses personification
- has vivid images, created using simile, metaphor and interesting synonyms
- uses poetic techniques, e.g. *alliteration, repetition.*

Grammar:

- my poem is written in free verse, so I have used line breaks instead of commas to show the reader where to pause when reading aloud.

See the Planning section of the Software ('Timetables' tab) for a printable version of the Writing purpose and evaluation.

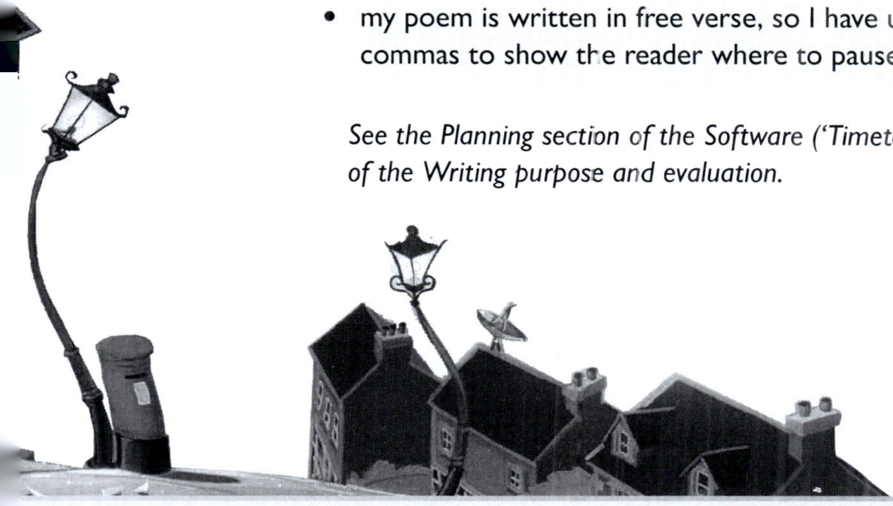

Fiction: Poetic style 'Last Night, I Saw The City Breathing' by Andrew Fusek Peters

READING FICTION

Resources
PB Pupils' Book, pp.26–35
A Anthology, pp.31–37
CD CD on interactive whiteboard, Unit 3
GB Grammar Bank on CD
HB Homework Book, pp.10–13

DAY 1

Curriculum link: read and discuss an increasingly wide range of poetry

The poetry store (CD)

Purpose: for children to develop an awareness of how poets use language to recreate real or imagined experiences

- Explain that poetry helps people to capture experiences and share them with others through the power of language. Tell the children that an artist recreates experience in picture form using paint and the poet does the same thing but uses language.
- Use the **CD (file 1.1)** to show extracts of poems on the theme of 'cities' and the whole poem 'Goodnight Stroud'. Read them to the children *briefly* explaining any tricky words and phrases – the point is to immerse the children in the poems and imagery rather than give detailed explanations.
- Tell the children they are now going to hear the bare bones of another poem about a city.

Introducing the poem 1 (CD)

Purpose: for children to become familiar with the bare bones of 'Last Night, I Saw The City Breathing'

- Read this introduction to the poem aloud all the way through to the children.

Introducing the poem 1

In a city at night there are people, trains, takeaways, cinemas and houses. There are brick walls, trees and avenues plus office blocks and parking lots. Houses, streets and roads have windows, roofs and lamps and a wind may be blowing through the city as it sleeps.

- Use MT/YT (My turn/Your turn), and TTYP (Turn to your partner) for each point (breaking the sentences into shorter sections if necessary). This is to help the children 'hold' the basic idea in their heads. Now display Introducing the poem 1 on the **CD (file1.2)** for the children to read.

identifying how language, structure and presentation contribute to meaning

Introducing the poem 2 (CD)

Before the lesson, you may wish to watch the video demonstrating Read a story version 1 (with a Year 5 story). This can be found in the Extras section of the software.

Purpose: for children to examine how Introducing the poem 2 provides additional information and for children to become more familiar with the ideas and images before they hear the full version

- Read Introducing the poem 2 to the children.

Introducing the poem 2

The city at night seems to be breathing as people are rushing in and out of a train station. It is as if the station is singing while the takeaways, cinemas and houses are laughing. There are shadows on brick walls and as trains are going in and out of the station, the trees seem to be performing.
The avenue, office blocks and parking lots are described as being hungry, fat and empty while windows are cracked.
There are paved streets, roads and street lamps and the wind is curling round the nooks of the roofs.

- Re-read it, using exaggerated intonation and expression. Stop after each section to ask the children if there are any words that tell them more about the city and what happens in the poem. TTYP and take feedback.
- Now display Introducing the poem 2 on the **CD (file 1.3)**. Click 'Highlights' to identify the additional information:
  - addition of the adjectives and more interesting verbs: *breathing, rushing, singing, laughing, performing, hungry, fat, empty, cracked, paved, curling*
  - addition of information about where the people rush to and from and the fact that there are shadows on the brick walls
- TOL (Think out loud) and use TTYP to share how this extra information changes the pictures in our minds as we hear the poem.

Curriculum link: making comparisons, identifying themes

Think and link 1

Purpose: for children to make links and connections with other poems and their own experiences

- Use TOL as you read through Introducing the poem 2 displayed on the **CD (file 1.4)**, encouraging children to think about their own experiences and connect to other poems they know. See **CD (file 1.5)** for a printable script of the TOL below.

'I wonder if the city at night is a scarier place or a more exciting place than it is in the day...

'Have you ever imagined that a place is alive and "breathing"? I always think that trees are alive when I walk in woods on my own. Perhaps we only feel or think these kinds of things when we are alone?

'The description of houses that "are laughing" reminds me of the line from the Wordsworth poem "the very houses seem asleep". Both of these lines make it seem as though the houses are alive!

'I wonder what the "paved streets" and "roads" are like. In Goodnight Stroud, Pie Corbett describes streets as "dark" and "restless". William Vaughan Moody writes about a "roaring street" that is "hung for miles/With fierce electric fire". What might the "fierce electric fire" be?

'What thoughts and feelings have you had about a city? When have you been in a city at night?'

- Use TTYP and take feedback to allow children to articulate and share ideas/connections and for you to paraphrase, clarify and extend their thoughts and ideas.

provide reasoned justifications for their views

Daily log

Purpose: for children to be introduced to the process of keeping a personal log of notes, thoughts and ideas, collected from their reading and discussions, to use in their own writing (see notes in Unit 1 Day 1, p.24 if necessary)

- Ask the children to TTYP to discuss the three descriptions in Introducing the poem 2 on the **CD (file 1.6)**, saying which they each like the best so far and why.
- Tell them to write at least one more line about a city at night using a simile.

effective discussion; provide justifications for their views

Big Question

Purpose: for children to develop their skills of argument and discussion through a mini enquiry session based on a philosophical question relating to the work of the day

- Display today's Big Question on the **CD (File 1.7)**:

Can a city breathe?

- Ask the children to TTYP to discuss. Collect feedback from partners and scribe some responses. Tell the children that each day's Big Question and their thoughts will be put in a safe place until the end of Week 2. They will then vote on which question to discuss more deeply. See Introduction for further notes (p.13).

DAY 2

Curriculum link: exploring the meaning of words in context

Word power 1

Purpose: for children to increase their knowledge of and application of synonyms and to examine how writers use language for effect

dashing	*hurrying*	*hurtling*	*cackling*	*chuckling*	*giggling*
charging	*scuttling*	*tearing*	*sniggering*	*chortling*	*laughing*
scooting	*rushing*		*doubling up*	*falling about*	

- Tell the children that there are lots of different words that mean the same as the word 'rushing' in Introducing the poem 2. Tell them that these *synonyms* can show different ways of rushing.
- Display the opening sentence from Introducing the poem 2 on the **CD (file 2.1)** and click 'Synonyms' to display synonyms for the word 'rushing'. Try swapping the word 'rushing' in Introducing the poem 2 for some of the synonyms, e.g. People *scooting* in and out of a train station.
- Now look at the second sentance and click 'Synonyms' to display synonyms for the word 'laughing'. Try swapping the word 'laughing' in Introducing the Poem 2 for some of the synonyms, e.g. *takeaways, cinemas and houses are sniggering.*
- TOL and use TTYP to share an example of how these words change the pictures in our minds as we hear them.
- Print all of these words from the **CD (file 2.2)** and display on your Poetry wall.

predicting

Think and link 2

Purpose: for children to develop their visualisation and predictive skills

- TOL: '*We don't know the whole poem yet but we can use our imagination to predict how some of the images might be developed by the writer.*'
- Display Introducing the poem 2 on the **CD (file 2.3)** and read out the words 'There are shadows on brick walls'.
- TOL: '*I wonder what the shadows will be of? I think they could be of other buildings. Or perhaps of night creatures – a city fox or a rat rummaging for food in bins? Maybe the writer won't tell us and then we will all imagine our own shadow shapes?*'
- Read out the words 'office blocks and parking lots are described as being hungry, fat and empty' from Introducing the poem 2.
- TOL: '*Why would the office blocks be described as fat? What are they packed with?*' Ask children to TTYP and take feedback. Encourage them to think beyond the obvious. Paraphrase, talk about and show how valuable and valid their ideas are.
- Repeat the process with the words 'paved streets' (TOL: '*What might the streets be paved with?*') and then 'dreaming roads' (TOL: '*What would a road be dreaming of?*')

Curriculum link: read and discuss an increasingly wide range of poetry, check the poem makes sense to them

Introducing the poem 3

Purpose: for children to hear and enjoy the full version of the poem for the first time

- Tell the children they are now going to hear the whole poem called 'Last Night, I Saw The City Breathing' by Andrew Fusek Peters for the very first time. TOL about which parts you can't wait to hear about, etc.
- Read the poem from the Anthology pp.32–33 to the children with great enjoyment, and appropriate intonation to really engage them.
- At the end of the poem, ask the children to TTYP to discuss the Introducing the poem 3 questions in the Pupils' Book p.26. Then collect feedback.

identifying and discussing themes

Daily log

Purpose: for children to develop their thinking and recording skills by logging their initial response to the whole poem

- Take one of the children's responses to one of the questions in the Introducing the poem 3 activity in the Pupils' Book p.26 and TOL as you model on the board how you could record this in a Daily log, using different stem sentences, e.g. '*I think the poem is serious and funny because… The poet has managed to make this poem both serious and funny by…*'
- Explain that they are going to record at least one of the ideas they discussed with their partners. Tell them to TTYP to share what they are going to record. Ask them to say their opening sentence to their partner before writing it down.

effective discussion; provide justifications for their views

Big Question

Purpose: for children to develop their skills of argument and discussion through a mini enquiry session based on a philosophical question relating to the work of the day

- Display today's Big Question on the **CD (File 2.4)**:

  Is it important to have poets in the world?

- Follow the process as explained at the end of Day 1 (p.69).

DAY 3

exploring the meaning of words in context

Word power 2

Purpose: for children to learn the meaning of rare vocabulary and discuss how these words and phrases are used in this story

gusts *split their sides* *creased themselves* *gloated* *boasted*

- Before the lesson, print all of the Power words and their synonyms from the **CD (file 3.1)** and display on your Poetry word wall.
- Look at the words and their definitions with the children and then read the sentences to them. Ask the children to repeat the sentences using MT/YT giving dramatic emphasis and actions as you say them.
- Find opportunities to use the words yourself throughout the day, e.g. 'I almost *split my sides* when I read your funny story!', 'I know we shouldn't *boast*, but we have done fantastic work today.'
- Encourage them to use the words at home with friends and family so that they become embedded in the children's own spoken (and eventually, written) vocabulary.
- Now tell the children to do the Word power 2 activity in the Pupils' Book p.26.

Curriculum link: exploring the meaning of words in context

Special phrases

Purpose: for children to revise some poetic features and become familiar with Special phrases particular to the poem

Last night, I saw the city breathing...

Last night, I saw the city laughing...

Last night, I saw the city dancing...

And the trees in the breeze...

Snaking Avenue smacked her lips, And swallowed seven roundabouts!

And the wind, Like a cat, Snoozed in the nooks of roofs.

- Display the Special phrases from the poem on the **CD (file 3.2)**.
- Explain that you have chosen these because they are phrases that we don't use in our everyday talk and also because they have some important poetic features. Read the phrases out loud.
- Now TOL (plan these ahead) as you draw attention to poetic features of some of the phrases that you like: repetition, rhyme, rhythm, alliteration, simile, metaphors, rhythm of the words, sound of the words together. You can use your own ideas or print out the TOL notes from the **CD (file 3.3)** for you to use as a script.
- Now ask the children to TTYP to read the Special phrases and the poetic features, given in the Pupils' Book p.27.

checking that the poem makes sense to them

Read the poem

Purpose: for children to gain a deeper understanding of the poem and to read the text for the first time

- Let the children follow their own copy of the poem in the Anthology pp.32–33 as you re-read the full version of the poem aloud with great enthusiasm.
- Now ask the children to read their copy of the poem with their partners, alternate stanzas each, and to read the words and phrases in bold with great expression. Explain that you will be listening in.

discuss and evaluate how authors use language, considering the impact on the reader

Daily log

Purpose: for children to keep a personal reading, writing and thinking log to record thoughts and ideas for their own writing

- Ask the children to decide on their favourite Power words and/or Special phrases from the poem in the Anthology pp.32–33 and why they like them. Ask them to TTYP to share and then record in their Daily log.

effective discussion; provide justifications for their views

Big Question

Purpose: for children to develop their skills of argument and discussion through a mini enquiry session based on a philosophical question relating to the work of the day

- Display today's Big Question on the **CD (file 3.4)**:

  Should natural environments be destroyed to make way for buildings for humans?*

- Follow the process as explained at the end of Day 1 (p.69).

**This Big Question will be revisited on Day 11 – the first day of the Non-fiction week.*

DAY 4

Curriculum link: read silently

Re-read the poem A

Purpose: for children to deepen their understanding of the poem by increasing familiarity with the text

- Ask the children to read the whole poem silently from the Anthology pp.32–33. Tell them to stop to record any thoughts, ideas, questions, or favourite bits in their Daily log as they read the text. Explain that it is more important for them to think about what they are reading than to finish first.

identifying how language contributes to meaning, learning the technical terms needed for discussing what they hear and read

Personification 1 CD PB A

Purpose: for children to be able to identify and explore the power of personification

- Use the **CD (file 4.1)** to show the word 'personification'. Ask the children to TTYP to see if they can spot the word within the word. Click 'Highlights' to highlight the word 'person' within 'personification' and to reveal further information.
- Explain that *personification* means giving *human* characteristics to a *non-human* object.
- Tell the children that lots of writers use personification in their poems. Use the **CD (file 4.2)** to show these examples from 'Goodnight Stroud':

The Clock Tower glowers. Dark streets yawn. …the night thinks…

- Read them out loud giving dramatic emphasis and actions as you say them. Ask the children to repeat each phrase and action using MT/YT and TTYP.
- Explain that personification helps writers to create powerful pictures and strong emotions for readers using just a few words.
- Tell the children that 'Clock Tower' is the noun that shows us the non-human object and 'glowers' is the verb that shows a human action. Ask the children to TTYP to identify the non-human object and the human action in the other two phrases. Check their understanding.
- Now show 'Last Night, I Saw the City Breathing' on the **CD (file 4.3)**. Explain that this poem is packed with personification!
- Use **CD (file 4.4)** to display the Personification grid for lines 1, 6, 10, 16, 21 and 24 showing the human action verbs for the non-human object 'city'.
- Now ask the children to TTYP and do the Personification activity in the Pupils' Book p.28, matching the non-human objects in the poem to the human actions. Tell them to check their answers by looking at the poem in the Anthology pp.32–33.
- Collect feedback, referring to the Anthology and display the Personification grid on the **CD (file 4.5)**. Use drag and drop to match the nouns and verbs

Non-human object (noun)		Human actions (verb)
Line 13 & 15	trees	put on a show
Line 25	roads	night-dreamed
Line 12	trains	wiggled their hips
Line 7	takeaways	got the giggles
Line 26	street lamps	boasted
Line 17	Snaking Avenue	smacked her lips

discuss and evaluate how authors use language

Personification 2 CD

Purpose: for children to be able to identify and explore the impact of writers' choices on the reader

- Show the **CD (file 4.6)** and consider the impact of the writer's use of personification by reading the example from the 'Image works well because…' section of the grid ("trees" and "roads"). TOL to let the children 'see' your thought processes. Don't make it look too easy. Hesitate and ask yourself questions and answer them yourself.

- Now bring the children into the TOL as you consider the impact of the other examples of personification. Ask them to TTYP to share their own thoughts and ideas. Stress the importance of trying out ideas. Remind children that there are no correct answers, just their own opinions. Type responses in the 'Image works well because...' column of the grid. Examples are given in **CD (file 4.7)** if you need them.

Curriculum link: summarising ideas

Daily log

Purpose: *for children to keep a personal reading, writing and thinking log to record thoughts and ideas for their own writing*

- Ask the children to draw a mind map of two or three of their favourite stanzas. Remind them to use a combination of pictures or symbols and words or phrases from the poem.

effective discussion; provide justifications for their views

Big Question (CD)

Purpose: *for children to develop their skills of argument and discussion through a mini enquiry session based on a philosophical question relating to the work of the day*

- Display today's Big Question on the **CD (file 4.8):**

  How would the way we live be different if buildings had feelings?

- Follow the process as explained at the end of Day 1 (p.69).

DAY 5

identifying and discussing themes

Who says? (CD)

Purpose: *for children to develop their awareness of the writer's voice in a text and how similar themes can be presented in different forms*

- Use the **CD (file 5.1)** to display the extract from the poem 'Block City' from the Poetry store Day 1. Tell the children that the poem was written more than a hundred years ago by a very famous writer called Robert Louis Stevenson.
- Read the poem out loud with appropriate enthusiasm and intonation.
- Do a quick vocabulary check, briefly explaining the meaning of archaic or tricky words such as *roam, kirk* and *vessel.*
- Explain to the children that each line in the poem has the same rhythm. Use MT/YT to read lines 1 and 2 out loud and clap to the four-beat rhythm.
- Ask the children to TTYP and repeat with lines 3 and 4.
- Tell the children that each pair of lines rhyme at the end. Click 'Highlights' to show the end rhymes.
- TOL about the effect of the regular rhythm and regular rhyme in 'Block City'. Use your own ideas as well as the think bubbles on the **CD (file 5.2)** and ask the children to TTYP to share ideas.
- Now use the **CD (file 5.3)** to show the poem 'Last Night, I Saw the City Breathing'. Tell the children that the writer, Andrew Fusek Peters, wrote the poem just a few years ago.
- Explain that he chose to write about a city as well but made very different choices to Robert Louis Stevenson about how the poem would look and sound.
- TOL as you point out the:
  - irregular rhythm
  - irregular rhyme – some at the ends of lines and some in the middle of lines
  - irregular shape on the page – explain that this is called 'free verse'. It is free from the 'rules' of a strict rhyme and rhythm pattern.

- Show the poem 'Goodnight Stroud' by Pie Corbett on the **CD (file 5.4)**. Read the poem out loud. Ask the children to TTYP to decide whether it is written in free verse or with a regular rhythm and rhyme pattern.
- Ask for evidence to support their answers. Collect feedback.

Curriculum link: identifying how presentation contributes to meaning

Dramatic reconstruction A PB

Purpose: for children to explore a writer's distinctive style through dramatic reconstruction; for children to develop a confident response to poems orally as a preparation for their own writing

- Organise the class into fours. Ask the children to look at the poem 'Last Night, I Saw The City Breathing' in the Anthology pp.32–33 and choose a stanza (remind the children that this means 'verse' if necessary) to perform.
- Explain that they can use actions, facial expression, sound effects, freeze-frames, body language in their performance.
- Remind them to vary the pace, volume and use pauses to create impact for their audience.
- Ask the children to use the prompts in the Dramatic reconstruction activity in the Pupils' Book p.28 to help them to create their performance.
- Allow time for the groups to plan and practise their performances. Walk around as they practise, giving instant feedback.

discuss their understanding of what they have read, provide reasoned justifications for their views

Daily log

Purpose: for children to keep a personal reading, writing and thinking log to record thoughts and ideas for their own writing

- Ask the children to record which one of the three poems they like best, giving at least three reasons.

effective discussion; provide justifications for their views

Big Question CD

Purpose: for children to develop their skills of argument and discussion through a mini enquiry session based on a philosophical question relating to the work of the day

- Display today's Big Question on the **CD (file 5.5)**:

  Can a pause or silence be more powerful than words?

- Follow the process as explained at the end of Day 1 (p.69).

WRITING FICTION

DAY 6

drawing inferences and justifying with evidence, identifying key details that support ideas

What if not...? PB CD

Purpose: for children to develop their ability to experiment with language and to consider the impact of changes made to a text

- Ask the children to look at the What if not...? questions in the Pupils' Book p.29. Model how you consider What if not...? for the first line of the poem 'Last Night, I Saw the City Breathing'. You can print the TOL script from the **CD (file 6.1)** or use your own ideas.
- Read the first line out loud and then ask children to repeat the line using MT/YT giving dramatic emphasis as you say it.
- Now ask the children to TTYP and discuss the other What if not...? questions. Collect feedback and build upon their ideas and changes as in the model example.

Curriculum link: understand through being shown the skills and processes essential for writing

Build an image

Purpose: for children to be able to build an image around one idea to bring the subject matter to life

- Use the **CD (file 6.2)** to show line 22 of the 'Last Night, I Saw the City Breathing' poem:

  Cracked windows poured falling stars.

- Read it out to the children. Ask the children to TTYP to discuss what pictures the words created in their heads. Ask for feedback. Explain that you really like the image of lots of pieces of glass from a broken window falling like stars.
- Now tell the children that you want to think of other ways of showing the same idea using different images.
- TOL: '*Would it work? Let's see…*'
  Offer an idea for a different image for the bits of broken glass falling from the cracked window:
  Cracked windows poured silver snowflakes
  Cracked windows poured sharp glitter
  and then ask the children to TTYP to share some ideas of their own.
- Tell the children that you are going to use the image of the *sharp glitter* because the snowflakes image is a bit too soft for broken glass. Say the line out loud and then ask children to repeat the line using MT/YT giving dramatic emphasis as you say it:

  Cracked windows poured sharp glitter

- Click 'New line' on the **CD (file 6.2)** to display the new line.
- Ask the children to say the new line using MT/YT.
- Display the line on the **CD (file 6.3)** and navigate through the CD to show the writing process allowing children to see writing in action.
- Explain that you can use the thesaurus to find other words that mean the same as *poured*. Click 'Synonyms' on the **CD (file 6.3)** to show these words:
  cascaded *sprinkled* *bombarded* *showered*
- Re-read the line, substituting synonyms for *poured*. Ask the children to show with thumbs up/down which ones they like. Tell the children that you like the word *showered* because it is another word that starts with the *sh* sound. Click on the **CD** to show this new line:

  Cracked windows showered sharp glitter.

- What about adding a simile? Say you like the poet's idea of the glass being like stars. What else could be like stars? Tiny meteorites! Click on the **CD** to show this new line:

  Cracked windows showered sharp glitter, like tiny meteorites.

- What about adding another adjective? Tell the children you could use *shiny* next to *tiny* to get a rhyme inside the line! Click on the **CD** to show this new line:

  Cracked windows showered sharp glitter, like tiny, shiny meteorites.

- Now ask the children, either individually or as partners, to compose their own line or lines out loud using the prompts in the Build an image activity in the Pupils' Book p.29. Do not let the children write until they can say their lines out loud. Once they have written them down, ask partners to take turns to develop each other's lines. Encourage crossings out, switching words round, etc. Emphasise that this is writing in action – it is not a neat, finished piece of writing!

Curriculum link: explain and discuss their understanding of what they have read

Daily log

Purpose: for children to keep a personal reading, writing and thinking log to record thoughts and ideas for their own writing

- Tell the children that they are going to hear a reading of the poem 'Goodnight Stroud'. Ask the children to listen carefully. Open the recording on the **CD (file 6.4)** to play a reading of the poem.
- Now ask them to record in their Daily log any words or phrases they can remember. Stress that it doesn't have to be accurate – just whatever they can recall!
- Now ask them to share and compare their words and discuss why they think they remembered those particular words or phrases.

effective discussion; provide justifications for their views

Big Question

Purpose: for children to develop their skills of argument and discussion through a mini enquiry session based on a philosophical question relating to the work of the day

- Display today's Big Question on the **CD (File 6.5)**:

  Why do people remember different things from the same experience?

- Follow the process as explained at the end of Day 1 (p.69).

DAY 7

plan their writing by using similar writing as models for their own

Build a poem 1

Purpose: for children to be able to see a poem grow through three stages of development

- Remind the children that for 'Last Night, I Saw The City Breathing' they heard Introducing the poem 1 and 2 before they heard and read the full poem. It *prepared* them to *read* the full poem.
- Tell the children to think back to the poems about cities they read earlier in the Unit, which inspired them to think about other places and what they are like at different times of the day. Say that you really like the contrast between a busy, bustling classroom full of children and that same room early in the morning before the children arrive.
- Display **CD (file 7.1)** to show the Build a poem 1 questions. Explain that they were the questions that helped the writer to know what to put in the new poem.
- Explain that you are going to show them two versions of a new poem to be written. These versions prepared the writer to write the full poem.
- Now display Build a Poem 1 on the **CD (file 7.2)**.
- Read out loud to the children. Explain that you are now going to show them another version of the new poem to be written. This one has additional information and words – it has been developed.

plan their writing by using other similar writing as models for their own

Build a poem 2

Purpose: for children to be able to see a poem grow through three stages of development

- Show Build a Poem 2 on the **CD (file 7.3)**. TOL as you compare this version with Build a poem 1. Click 'Highlights' to show examples of additional information, description and similes.

Build a poem 3

Purpose: for children to see an example of writing that will provide a model for their own writing

- Before the lesson, you will need to print one copy for each set of partners of **CD (file 7.5)**.

- Tell the children that you can now show them the full poem. (The poem is provided as a model for writing.)
- Display **CD (file 7.4)** to show the poem. Explain that when writing this poem, the poet was thinking about an empty classroom in the early morning. Read the poem (Build a poem 3) to the children.
- Give out one copy of the poem and evaluation questions for each set of partners from the **CD (file 7.5)**. Using TTYP and oral feedback, ask the children to evaluate the writing. Collect feedback.

Curriculum link: noting initial ideas

Daily log (CD)

Purpose: for children to keep a personal reading, writing and thinking log to record thoughts and ideas for their own writing

- Ask the children to look at their printed copy of Build a poem 3 from the **CD (file 7.5)** and then share ideas for a title for the poem. Ask them to record their best ideas in their Daily log and explain why they think they are good titles.

effective discussion; provide justifications for their views

Big Question (CD)

Purpose: for children to develop their skills of argument and discussion through a mini enquiry session based on a philosophical question relating to the work of the day

- Display today's Big Question on the **CD (File 7.6)**:

  If something is given a name, does it change what it is?

- Follow the process as explained at the end of Day 1 (p.69).

DAY 8

understand through being shown, the skills and processes essential for writing

Write a poem 1 (CD)

Purpose: for children to develop their confidence and skills in poetry planning and development

- Tell the children that they are going to write their own poem about a classroom after school.
- Use these guide questions and TTYP to stimulate the children's imagination about a classroom after school – the examples in brackets are just suggestions if their ideas stall:
  - What might the classroom *look* like straight after the children have gone? (The furniture? The whiteboard? Things left behind?)
  - What sounds might be *heard?* (Computers humming? Vacuums cleaning? Class pet rustling in its cage?)
  - What might it *smell* like? (Wax crayons? Polish? Musty carpets? Glue?)
  - Personify the classroom – what might it *feel* like?
- Walk around and listen in, praising good quality discussions.
- Collect feedback, expanding on and recording their ideas in note form on the board.
- Now display **CD (file 8.1)** for the children to read to show them the pre-prepared 'bare bones' version of a poem about a classroom after school.

Write a poem 2 (CD) (PB)

Purpose: for children to develop their confidence and skills in poetry planning and development

- Explain that you are going to borrow some of the *poetic features* in 'Goodnight Stroud' and 'Last Night, I Saw the City Breathing' and use them to develop line 1.
- Display the **CD (file 8.2)** to show the process of creating and crafting the poem, and use the think bubbles and your own ideas to TOL. Encourage the children to offer their opinions and ideas.

- Ask the children to work with their partners to develop line 2 using the prompts in the Write a poem 2 activity in the Pupils' Book p.30, experimenting through making changes and discussing the effects of the changes.
- Remind them to keep saying the line out loud to each other to hear the effects of the sounds and rhythm of the words.
- Emphasise the fact that they are experimenting with language – there is not a right answer.
- Now display **CD (file 8.3)** to show the developed version of line 3.
- Guide children to identify features that show the development and use of poetic features such as personification, alliteration, simile, line breaks, sounds of words close together, rhyme or half rhyme.
- Ask the children to develop line 4 of Write a poem 1, **CD (file 8.1)** on their own, using the prompts in the Pupils' Book p.30.

Curriculum link: noting and developing initial ideas

Daily log

Purpose: for children to keep a personal reading, writing and thinking log to record thoughts and ideas for their own writing

- Ask the children to write a list of as many words or phrases as possible to do with classrooms at any time of the day or night and turn it into a list poem.

effective discussion; provide justifications for their views

Big Question

Purpose: for children to develop their skills of argument and discussion through a mini enquiry session based on a philosophical question relating to the work of the day

- Display today's Big Question on the **CD (file 8.4)**:

  Can you only learn in a classroom?

- Follow the process as explained at the end of Day 1 (p.69).

DAY 9

describing settings and atmosphere

Write a poem 3

Purpose: for children to use the lines they have already developed to write their own poem

- Tell the children that they are ready to write their own free verse poem about a classroom after school. Ask them to continue to use the poetry prompts in the Write a poem 2 activity in the Pupils' Book p.30 and any useful parts of the Anthology or Daily log to help them. Remind them to look at the Poetry wall for Power words and phrases and a thesaurus for synonyms.
- Encourage children to rehearse their ideas with their partners before they begin to write.
- Remind them to be willing to make changes and play with the sounds and rhythm of words.
- You may wish to display the developed lines you modelled with the children on the **CD** on Day 8.

DAY 10

perform their own compositions, assessing the effectiveness of their own and others' writing

Share a poem

Purpose: for children to read and share their full poems

- Ask the children to read through their own poem, underlining their favourite or best parts. Ask them to share these with their partners. Collect feedback on best bits from partners.
- Make sure that any powerful or rarer words or phrases are written on card and added to the Poetry wall.

Curriculum link: assessing the effectiveness of their own and others' writing

Evaluate and edit (CD)

Purpose: for children to evaluate their own and their partner's work against specific criteria and then discuss how they could improve their work

- Display **CD (file 10.1)** to show the evaluation prompts and read them together using MT/YT.
- As a model, select an example of work from the children where the writing has met the criteria, and share this with the other children, explaining why it works well.
- Tell the children to take turns to read their partner's writing and discuss how well they have met the criteria.
- Ask children to discuss at least two changes they could make to improve their work following the partner discussion.

proofread for spelling and punctuation errors

Proofread

Purpose: for children to proofread their work and make changes to improve the accuracy of their grammar, punctuation and spelling

- Now ask the children to proofread their work. If you have noticed that several children need to improve on a particular aspect of spelling, grammar or punctuation, use this as a focus for the Proofread activity. Write an example which includes common errors from the children's writing and use this as a model.
- The children should always be checking for standard use of punctuation and correct spelling of common exception words.
- The following points would be relevant as the particular focus for this Unit:
  - checking correct use of punctuation for effect
  - checking spelling of more ambitious vocabulary choices.

effective discussion; provide justifications for their views, distinguish between fact and opinion

Very Big Question (CD)

Purpose: for children to develop their willingness to broaden or revise their opinions through exploring one of the Big Questions in more depth

- See Unit 1 Day 10 for teaching notes on the Very Big Question (p.36).

Persuasive writing

READING AND WRITING NON-FICTION

The non-fiction part of the Unit explores persuasive writing and is linked to the 'cities' theme of the poetry. The children examine the audience and purpose of persuasive texts. They write a persuasive presentation which they present to the class in the role of residents at a public meeting to discuss plans for building a football stadium.

See p.66 for the daily timetable for the Non-fiction week.

Non-fiction

Reading

Children will:

- explore different forms of persuasive texts and consider when and why they are used
- understand that persuasive writing has a clear purpose and intended audience
- explore how opinions can be disguised as fact in order to persuade the reader.

Writing

Key writing purpose to be shared with the children:

To write a presentation persuading people to consider my point of view about whether or not there should be a new football stadium.

Writing evaluation to be shared with the children

My presentation:

- uses the ideas from my email and advert to put forward an argument about whether or not the stadium should be built
- puts my ideas across in a powerful and memorable way to persuade my reader, by using *rhetorical questions, commands and exaggerations, opinions disguised as fact*
- uses particular persuasive phrases to engage the reader's attention, e.g. *It's about time that… Don't even think that…*

Grammar:

- includes modal verbs, to show the possibility of something happening as a way of persuading my reader.

See the Planning section of the Software ('Timetables' tab) for a printable version of the Writing purpose and evaluation.

DAY 11

Curriculum link: to read and discuss a range of non-fiction

Introduction

Purpose: for children to revise their existing knowledge of persuasive texts using the context of one of the Big Questions and the poetry texts studied in Weeks 1 and 2

- Show the Big Question from Day 3 on the **CD (file 3.4)**: *Should natural environments be destroyed to make way for buildings for humans?*
- Ask the children to TTYP to recall some of the thoughts and ideas they had in their discussion. Collect feedback.
- Remind the children that the poems they have been reading and writing link strong human emotions to places and buildings.
- Display on the **CD (file 11.1)** the quotations from Lord Byron and John Milton from Day 1 to show opposite points of view about natural and man-made environments.
- Ask the children to TTYP to say which poet likes cities and which one doesn't.
- Explain that when we have a point of view about something we really care about, we might try to persuade people to agree with us.
- Tell the children that if Lord Byron had met John Milton, he might have tried to persuade or convince Milton that cities were 'torture' by encouraging him to see his point of view!
- Explain that a point of view or 'opinion' can have additional information to make it more persuasive. Read these examples out loud with appropriate emphasis and intonation or make up your own:

  '"The hum of human cities is torture" because you can never switch it off!'

  '"Towered cities please us" and "the busy hum of men" shows that humans are happily working together!'
- Display **CD (file 11.2)** to show the statements below. Ask the children to TTYP to add information to these statements to make them more persuasive:
  - *My pocket money should go up now* because…
  - *I think we should go to the park today* because…
- Collect examples from partners and use MTYT to show how facial expression, body language and intonation is used to present points of view or arguments convincingly.
- Remind the children that when we want to persuade someone in written form, the reader can't see us so we have to use the features of persuasive writing.
- Say that you have found an old letter that seems to be trying to persuade someone that the city is a great place. Display **CD (file 11.3)**. Read the letter out loud to the children.
- Now ask them to discuss with their partner: 'Would this letter persuade Sam to visit the city?' Remind the children to have reasons to support their answers.
- Collect feedback. Explain that:
  - once we write something down it is called a text
  - persuasive texts have certain features
  - the letter to Sam is one example of a *persuasive text.*
- Ask the children to TTYP to think of different types of writing that persuade us to do something, believe something or want something, e.g. adverts, arguments for or against something in letters or formal essays, use of statistics, graphs, etc.,in reports to support a point of view, film clips and song lyrics used as propaganda, placards in protest marches.

exploring the meaning of words in context

Word power

Purpose: for children to become familiar with some words and synonyms associated with persuasive texts

persuade   fact   opinion   command   rhetorical questions

- Before the lesson, print all of these words and their definitions from the **CD (file 11.4)**.
- Show them to the children and explain that they are words that will help us to identify and write persuasive texts.
- Now read these sentences to the children. Ask the children to repeat the sentences using MT/YT.

  persuade: 'Mum tried to *persuade* me to eat more vegetables!'
  fact: 'It is a *fact* that I danced at the party.'
  opinion: 'In my *opinion*, I am a brilliant dancer!'
  command: 'I *command* you to do it now!'
  rhetorical questions: 'What on earth do you think you are doing? No, don't tell me, it was a *rhetorical question!*'
- Display words and definitions on your Non-fiction wall. The children must hear, see and repeat the words in your teaching and conversation throughout the day, e.g.

  'Oh dear, I thought I could *persuade* you to pack away quietly!'

  'It is a well known *fact* that we have maths after break today.'

  'There is no right answer to this – it is your *opinion* that counts!'

  'I'm not going to *command* you to do it, I am going to ask you nicely!'

  You could ask the children to notice when you ask a rhetorical question during the day.
- Now tell the children to do the Word power activity in the Pupils' Book p.31.

Curriculum link: learn the conventions of different types of writing

Persuasive texts (CD)

Purpose: for children to be able to recognise the basic structure and features of persuasive texts

- Display **CD (file 11.5)** to show the examples of different persuasive texts. Read them out loud.
- Now TOL, drawing the children into the process as you use the Highlighter tool on your whiteboard to identify examples of these key features of persuasive writing:
  - phrases to make people feel silly if they don't agree
  - phrases to make you think everyone else agrees
  - words and phrases to make you want something
  - rhetorical questions
  - facts
  - opinions
  - exaggerations
  - information that might be true but is hard to check
  - commands – 'Do it now!'

identifying the audience for and purpose of the writing

Audience and purpose (CD) (PB)

Purpose: for children to be able to recognise that the form of persuasive texts will vary to suit different audiences and purpose

- Keep the extracts on the **CD (file 11.5)** and TOL as you spot clues that help you to identify the probable purpose and target audience (reader) of Text A. Use these prompts if you need to:

  TOL: 'Hmm, this seems to be some sort of school newsletter. It addresses 'parents and carers' and asks them to talk to their children. So I think the form of it is a newsletter and the purpose is to persuade parents and carers to talk to their children about dropping litter. The target reader or audience must be the parents and carers then.'

- Now ask the children to find the Audience and purpose activity in the Pupils' Book pp.32–33 and look at the texts and list of possible audiences. Tell them to TTYP to discuss and then choose the probable audience of the other texts, e.g. a pet owner = text B? C? D? Remind them that they should be able to explain their choices. N.B. An additional text (D) is included in the Pupils' Book to make the task more challenging.
- Collect feedback and clarify.

Curriculum link: noting initial ideas, drawing on reading and research

Daily log

Purpose: for children to keep a personal reading, writing and thinking log to record thoughts and ideas for their own writing

- Tell the children that over the next few days, you want them to look in magazines, newspapers, the Internet or packaging for examples of persuasive writing of any kind. Ask them to bring them to school to stick them in their Daily log. Tell them to write a note next to each one of where they found it. Tell them to make sure they are not *all* from the Internet!

DAY 12

using other similar writing as models for their own

Deconstruction 1 (CD) A

Purpose: for children to see an example of writing that will provide a model for the planning of their own writing

- Tell the children that a local town has just heard about plans to build a new football stadium, shopping mall, leisure centre and car park on a local beauty spot that has a children's play area, a skateboard park, a lake and a woodland walk. The old football stadium in the town centre will be demolished.
- Display the **CD (file 12.1)** to show pictures of the local beauty spot and its amenities.
- Now ask them to TTYP to share their first thoughts about building on this land. Collect feedback.
- Explain that some people from the town are so angry that they are holding a residents' meeting to plan how to stop the building work.
- Ask the children to find the 'Meet the Monster!' text in the Anthology pp.34–35. Tell them to follow the text as you read it out loud with lots of expression.
- Explain that this is an advert to *persuade* people to attend the meeting. Ask them to TTYP and read the text, reading alternate sections each.
- Now ask the children to discuss with their partners how effective the advert is:
  - What are the best features of the advert?
  - What could improve the advert?
- Collect feedback.

Year 5 Grammar indicating degrees of possibility using adverbs

Grammar: adverbs of possibility (CD)

Purpose: for children to recognise how adverbs can be used to indicate degrees of possibility

- Write the word 'adverb' on the board. Use MY/YT to say the word. Display the **CD (file 12.2)** to show a definition and some examples. Read the definition aloud using MT/YT. Look at the examples together, then click 'TOL' and use the TOL bubbles to explain how you know which words are the adverbs.
- Tell the children that you are going to look at a special group of adverbs, which describe things that haven't happened yet, but might happen in the future. (If appropriate, say that these can be referred to as 'adverbs of possibility'.)

- Click to the next slide and use MT/YT to read the words: *perhaps, maybe, possibly*. Remind the children that these adverbs are used when talking about things that might happen in the future.
- Read the examples using MT/YT and then ask the children to TTYP and make up a sentence of their own, using the adverb 'perhaps'. You could start them off by making up another sentence of your own, e.g. '*Perhaps* one day we will all like adverbs!'
- Take feedback, then ask them to do the same with 'maybe' and 'possibly'. Encourage imaginative speculations as well as sensible ones, e.g. 'Maybe one day we will all live on Mars!'
- Explain that there are other adverbs that we use to describe things that are much more likely to happen in the future. Click to the next slide and use MT/YT to read the words *certainly, definitely, surely*. Encourage the children to say these words in a strong, determined voice, to emphasise that they show something is certain to happen.
- Read the examples with the children using MT/YT. Emphasise how these adverbs describe something that is very likely to happen, rather than just a vague possibility. Again, ask the children to TTYP to think up example sentences of their own, then share them with the class.

Curriculum link: using organisational and presentational devices to structure text and to guide the reader

Write a persuasive text 1 PB CD A

Purpose: for children to develop their confidence and skills in planning and creating an advert using an example of writing that will provide a model for their own writing

- Explain that the way information is presented in adverts is important.
- Ask the children to look at **text D,** the advert for a pet hotel in the Fupils' Book p.33.
- Now display **CD (file 12.3)** to show a developed version of the pet hotel advert.
- Identify the addition of pictures, bullet points, boxed text and extra information and ask the children to TTYP to discuss the effectiveness of the organisation and layout of the revised advert.
- Tell the children they are going to make similar changes to the advert for the residents' meeting so that it has greater impact and more persuasive power!
- Explain that they are going to create their own advert for the meeting.
- Remind them to use the 'Meet the Monster.' text in the Anthology pp.34–35 plus the pet advert and prompts on the **CD (file 12.4)** to help them.
- Tell the children to TTYP to share ideas before starting their advert.

provide reasoned justifications for their views

Daily log

Purpose: for children to keep a personal reading, writing and thinking log to record thoughts and ideas for their own writing

- Tell the children to think of at least two reasons why the building of the new football stadium, shopping mall, leisure centre and car park on a beauty spot should *not* go ahead. Ask them to write them as bullet points in their Daily log under the heading 'Against'.

DAY 13

Curriculum link: distinguish between statements of fact and opinion

Deconstruction 2 (CD) (A) (print)

Purpose: for children to be able to identify facts and opinions in a text and analyse how they can be used to manipulate and persuade

- Before the lesson, you will need to print one Fact and opinion grid for each set of partners from the **CD (file 13.1)**.
- Tell the children that Denton United football club has sent out flyers to all homes and businesses in the town to inform them of their plans and to persuade them to support the building work.
- Ask the children to find the flyer in the Anthology pp.36–37. Tell them to follow the text as you read it aloud with lots of expression.
- Now ask the children to read it with their partners, reading alternate paragraphs each.
- Explain that there are some facts and some opinions in the text. Some of the opinions are disguised as facts. Point to the fact and opinion definitions on your Persuasive writing wall and use MT/YT to revise them.
- Now display **CD (file 13.2)** to show the facts and opinions grid. Show and explain the three examples given.
- Give each set of partners their printed copy of the grid and tell the children to TTYP to complete the rest of the grid together.
- Collect answers orally. Type into the cells to complete the grid on the CD. Clarify points and generate discussion, using TTYP, about manipulation of facts and opinions to persuade, e.g. half-truths, bias or opinions that appear to be facts.

using other similar writing as models for their own

Persuasive language (CD) (A)

Purpose: for children to investigate the use of persuasive language in a text and to use it as a model for their own writing

- Display the Denton United flyer on the **CD (file 13.3)**. Use TOL to identify examples of persuasive language:
  - phrases to make the reader feel silly if they don't agree
  - phrases to create trust in the reader
  - words and phrases to make you want something
  - words and phrases to make you feel strong emotions
  - rhetorical questions
  - exaggerations
  - commands and imperatives such as 'Do it now!'
- Now display **CD (file 13.4)** to show think bubbles. Use these and/or use your own analysis to TOL as you analyse the effect of the persuasive language.

Year 5 Grammar indicating degrees of possibility using modal verbs

Grammar: modal verbs (CD) (PB) (HB)

Purpose: for children to recognise how modal verbs can be used to indicate degrees of possibility

- Say to the children that the Denton United flyer mentions the certainty of what it will bring to the community. Display the **CD (file 13.5)** to show an extract.
- Tell the children that you want to look closely at the verbs. If necessary, remind them that the verbs are words that describe what someone or something is doing, and that you can recognise them because they have a tense, e.g. past, present or future. Ask the children to TTYP and pick out one of the verbs in the extract.
- Take feedback, then click to reveal the verb phrases. Point out that the main verbs are 'make sure' and 'sit', but there are little 'helping' verbs just before them, i.e. 'will' and 'can'. Explain that this sort of 'helping verb' is called a modal verb.

- Click to the next slide and use MT/YT to read out the complete list of modal verbs. The children could repeat them all like a chant.
- Tell the children that modal verbs are a bit like the adverbs they looked at earlier in the unit (Day 12) in that they can show how likely something, in the future, is to happen. Click to the next slide to display the three sentences. Ask the children to TTYP and decide which words are the modal verbs.
- Take feedback and click to highlight the modal verbs. TOL to show how the modal verbs give different levels of possibility.
- Ask the children to look at the Grammar: modal verbs activity on p.34 of their Pupils' Book. Tell them to TTYP to complete the activity orally. Ask them to feed back their answers clarifying where necessary.

Homework Book p.13 provides further practice on modal verbs.

Curriculum link:
writing non-fiction

Write a persuasive text 2

Purpose: for children to write a persuasive text

- Tell the children that they are ready to write their own persuasive text.
- Explain that they are in the role of an older child or a teenager living in Denton who is thrilled about the new Winmore stadium, leisure and shopping complex and worried that the plans might not go ahead.
- Ask the children to TTYP to write a letter or an email to the football club supporting the plan. Remind them to:
  - TTYP to discuss the main points they want to make
  - rehearse their opening sentence to their partner before they begin to write
  - use the prompts in the Write a persuasive text 2 activity in the Pupils' Book p.34 to help them
  - use any useful parts of their Daily log or the 'Meet the Future' text in the Anthology pp.36–37
  - use any useful parts of their Daily log.

proofread for spelling and punctuation errors

Proofread

Purpose: for children to proofread their work and make changes to improve the accuracy of their grammar, punctuation and spelling

- Now ask the children to proofread their work. If you have noticed that several children need to improve on a particular aspect of spelling, grammar or punctuation, use this as a focus for the Proofread activity. Write an example which includes common errors from the children's writing and use this as a model.
- The children should always be checking for standard use of punctuation and correct spelling of common exception words.
- The following points would be relevant as the particular focus for this Unit:
  - checking that the correct punctuation has been used, e.g. *rhetorical questions* and *commands*
  - checking for correct use of adverbs of possibility, e.g. *perhaps, maybe, definitely*
  - checking the correct spelling of more ambitious vocabulary

Curriculum link: developing ideas, provide reasoned justifications for their views

Daily log

Purpose: for children to keep a personal reading, writing and thinking log to record thoughts and ideas for their own writing

- Tell the children to add at least one more bullet point to their list of reasons why the stadium plan should *not* go ahead. Tell them to make a new heading 'For' and list at least three of their reasons for the stadium plan to go ahead.

DAY 14

explain and discuss their understanding of what they have read, including through debates

Deconstruction 3 PB CD

Purpose: for children to develop their understanding of how persuasive language can be adapted for different audiences and settings. For children to see how persuasive devices can be used in informal oral discussions and formal oral presentations

- Tell the children to TTYP and use the Deconstruction 3 activity in the Pupils' Book p.35 to act out a short role-play of people with opposite views about the Winmore stadium. Encourage them to use appropriate expression.
- Explain that as it is an informal discussion, the language is everyday spoken language.
- Display **CD (file 14.1)** to show the picture strip of the Denton's residents' public meeting.
- Read the speech bubbles out loud to the children with appropriate passion and intonation!
- Point out the modal verbs to show how likely things are to happen (see screen 4).
- TOL about the more formal format and language of the public meeting compared to the more colloquial language of their role-plays.

draft and write

Write a persuasive text 3 A PB

Purpose: for children to develop their understanding of how to construct an argument to persuade others and to present their point of view orally in a formal setting

- Ask the children to TTYP to decide whether they want to argue for or against the building of the Winmore Stadium, leisure complex and shopping mall.
- Explain that they are going to work on a short persuasive presentation of their point of view to be delivered to the whole group tomorrow.
- Tell them to use the lists of points they wrote in their Daily log as the basis for their presentations.
- Remind them to make notes of the points they will make and to work together to use some of the persuasive devices they have been looking at in the Anthology texts and the Pupils' Book.
- Remind them to use modal verbs where appropriate, e.g. *will, could, should, must.*
- Depending on the availability of ICT equipment and time, they could use PowerPoint in their presentations.

developing initial ideas, provide reasoned justifications for their views

Daily log

Purpose: for children to keep a personal reading, writing and thinking log to record thoughts and ideas for their own writing

- Ask the children to think about and record how their own views have changed or been made stronger by listening to, reading and writing about different points of view on the Winmore Stadium plan.

DAY 15

Curriculum link: explain and discuss their understanding of what they have read, including through formal presentations and debates, using notes where necessary

assessing the effectiveness of their own and others' writing

Persuasive presentations

Purpose: for children to complete and present their arguments for or against the stadium

- Allow time for the children to complete their presentation notes.
- Tell the children that they are going to present as if they were at the residents' meeting. Remind them about respecting each other's points of view and listening carefully to each other.
- Take the role of the neutral chairperson to 'open' the meeting and to chair it as the partners deliver their persuasive presentations in turn.
- At the end of all the presentations, tell the children that they are going to vote for or against the plan. Make sure they know that they can change their original views if they have been persuaded by other people's arguments.

Evaluate and edit (CD)

Purpose: for children to evaluate their own and their partner's work against specific criteria and then discuss how they could improve their work

- Display **CD (file 15.1)** to show the evaluation prompts and read them together using MT/YT.
- As a model, select an example of a presentation where the children met the criteria, and share with the other children why it worked well.
- Tell the children to discuss with their partner how well they met the criteria.
- Ask children to discuss at least two changes they could make to improve their presentation following the partner discussion.

Daily log

Purpose: for children to keep a personal reading, writing and thinking log to record thoughts and ideas for their own writing

- Ask the children to vote and then record the *fact* of the result in their Daily log with a brief note on their *opinion* of the result.

Unit 4

Fiction: Stories by significant children's authors
Non-fiction: Biography and autobiography

Timetable

WEEK 1 **Reading fiction** *This Is NOT a Fairy Tale*

Day 1	Day 2	Day 3	Day 4	Day 5
The story store	Read a story version 3	Word power	Grammar: parenthesis	Who says?
Read a story version 1	Clarify	Re-read a story version 3	Re-read a story version 3	Drama – in role, Luke and Ramona
Think and link	Think and link – map the story	Read and compare	Drama – zoom in	What if not...?
Read a story version 2	Daily log	Daily log	Daily log	Daily log
Daily log – predicting	Big Question	Big Question	Big Question	Big Question
Big Question				

WEEK 2 **Writing fiction** *This Is NOT a Fairy Tale*

Day 6	Day 7	Day 8	Day 9	Day 10
Build a sentence	Build an episode 1	Write a story 1 – plan	Write a story 3	Share a story
Tell a story	Build an episode 2	Write a story 2 – dialogue		Evaluate and edit
Daily log	Build an episode 3	Daily log		Proofread
Big Question	Daily log	Big Question		Very Big Question
	Big Question			

WEEK 3 **Reading and writing non-fiction** Biography and autobiography

Day 11	Day 12	Day 13	Day 14	Day 15
Linking the texts	Deconstruction 1	Deconstruction 2	Deconstruction 3	Evaluate and edit
Introduction	Read a biography	Build a biography – Top Tips for taking notes	Write a biography	Proofread
Key features				
Evaluating texts				
Daily log				

: shows that a file should be printed out from the Software.

Overview of the Unit

This Unit explores the work of the author Jeremy Strong, focusing on one of his short stories. The children are encouraged to use this and other examples of his work to find out about his style. They explore how he creates his stories as a series of humorous episodes with pace and excitement. The children use various techniques to help them understand how to create characters and dialogue. Supported by modelled texts and planning, they write their own episode that continues the story.

In the Non-fiction week the children examine the difference between biography and autobiography. For more information about the Non-fiction week and the Non-fiction writing evaluation criteria, see p.105.

The Homework Book provides a homework activity related to the content of this Unit for each of the three weeks.

Fiction

Reading

Children will:

- make links between stories by Jeremy Strong and their own experiences
- explore Jeremy Strong's style and techniques, e.g. *creating humour by subverting stereotypes*
- understand that the narrator has a point of view, and that this is revealed by the way the narrator describes the characters.

Writing

Key writing purpose to be shared with the children:

To use ideas from Jeremy Strong's stories to write a new episode of This is NOT a Fairy Tale, *in which Ramona meets a frightening character.*

Writing evaluation to be shared with the children

My story:

- uses what I know about Ramona to show how she acts
- has dialogue to move the story on and give new information about Ramona's feelings and hopes
- has jokes written in the style of Jeremy Strong.

Grammar:

- includes parenthesis to add extra comments to the story in the style of Jeremy Strong
- uses inverted commas to show the reader when a character is talking.

See the Planning section of the Software ('Timetables' tab) for a printable version of the Writing purpose and evaluation.

Fiction: Stories by significant children's authors
This is NOT a Fairy Tale by Jeremy Strong

READING FICTION

Resources
- PB Pupils' Book, pp.36–42
- A Anthology, pp.38–55
- CD CD on interactive whiteboard, Unit 4
- GB Grammar Bank on CD
- HB Homework Book, pp.14–16

DAY 1

Curriculum link: identifying and discussing themes and conventions, making comparisons within and across books

The story store (CD)

Purpose: *for children to understand who Jeremy Strong is and to contextualise the main themes of his work*

- Make a Jeremy Strong Book Corner to support this Unit and to give the children access to his work. More about the author and his work as well as downloads can be found on his website http://www.jeremystrong.co.uk/.
- Brainstorm any prior knowledge the children have of Jeremy Strong's books. Read some of the titles of his books and show the front covers. Ask the children to TTYP (Turn to your partner) and discuss their initial impression of his books.
- Display the summaries of three of his stories on the **CD (file 1.1)**.
- Draw the children's attention to the episodic nature of the stories. Break down one of the story summaries so that they can see the different episodes and how they build upon each other to create more misunderstandings, humour or excitement.
- Ask the children to look out for funny names and note them down. After you have read each summary ask the children to TTYP and discuss the funny names they have found and why they think they are funny. Explain that this is part of Jeremy Strong's writing style.
- Introduce the concept of stereotypical characters by talking about fairy tale characters;
  TOL (Think out loud): '*The princess is always beautiful and needs to be rescued. There is always a handsome prince.*'
  Then move on to other stereotypical characters.
  TOL: '*Grannies in stories often are kind and knit and aren't very adventurous but in* My Granny's Great Escape *Granny has married a Hell's Angel and causes all sorts of trouble. Jeremy Strong likes to turn stereotypes on their heads.*'
- Display one of the summaries and ask the children to TTYP and find a character that Jeremy Strong has created that breaks the stereotype. Take feedback.

read fiction

Read a story version 1 (CD)

Before the lesson, you may wish to watch the video demonstrating Read a story version 1. This can be found in the Extras section of the software.

Purpose: *for children to become familiar with Story 1, the bare bones of* This Is NOT a Fairy Tale

- Read aloud all the way through to the children – do not reveal the ending of the final story. Do not read the numbers aloud.

  Story version 1

  1. A young poor man lived with his mother and a dog in a poor village at the bottom of a mountain.
  2. All the villagers told old tales and thought themselves very wise.
  3. The young man realised the villagers weren't wise at all but full of nonsense, so he decided to use his brain and have an adventure.
  4. In a castle at the top of the mountain there was a princess trapped and waiting for a brave prince to rescue and marry her.

5. The young man wanted a companion on his adventures, so he thought he'd rescue the princess and travel with her.
6. The young man had to face many dangers before he could get to the princess.
7. The villagers gave him advice before he set off on his quest.
8. Luckily the young man ignored everything they said!

- Use MT/YT (My turn/Your turn) and TTYP for each point – you will need to break down the longer points! Use exaggerated intonation and emphasis where appropriate to make the sentences memorable. This will help the children to 'hold' the basic story in their heads.
- Now display Story version 1 on the **CD (file 1.2)** so the children can see the text and note how much of it they have remembered.

Curriculum link: making comparisons, identifying themes

Think and link

Purpose: for children to make links and connections with other Jeremy Strong stories

- Return to the other stories from the Story store on the **CD (file 1.1)** and link them to Story version 1. Ask the children to TTYP and see if they can find any stereotypical characters.
- Draw the children's attention to the fact that the young man would have to face many dangers. These could be the mini episodes Jeremy Strong uses in his stories to create humour and excitement.

predicting; identifying how language, structure, and presentation contribute to meaning

Read a story version 2

Purpose: for children to examine how Story version 2 provides additional information for the reader and for children to become more familiar with the story before they hear the full version

- Read Story version 2 (below) to the children. Explain that it has been developed.

Story version 2

1. Luke was a young man of eighteen and he lived with his mother, Old Crone, and his pet dog Shaggy in a poor ramshackle village at the bottom of a mountain.
2. There was nothing much to do in the evenings so the villagers amused themselves by telling old tales and sharing their wisdom. They thought themselves very wise.
3. Luke realised the villagers weren't wise at all. Their sayings such as "What I say is, before the last apple falls there'll be trouble," were nonsense so he decided to use his brain and have an adventure.
4. In a lonely castle at the top of the mountain there was a princess named Ramona who was as beautiful as the sunset. She was trapped and waiting for a brave prince to rescue and marry her.
5. Luke was bored with life in the village and wanted a companion on his adventures, so he thought he'd rescue the princess and travel the world with her.
6. The young man had to climb the mountain and face the many dangers that lurked there: the flesh tearing brambles, the Black Bear, the Waggletooth Witch, the Trolls of Tiddly Crag and the Giant Man-Eating Unicorn That Nobody Had Ever Seen before he could rescue the princess Ramona.
7. The villagers gave him advice like "When the Black Bear tries to eat you, rub your skin with acorn juice and hiss. Then the bear will vanish!" before he set off on his quest.
8. Luckily the young man ignored everything they said!

- Now display Story version 2 on the **CD (file 1.3)**. Click 'Highlights' to show how the story has changed.
- TOL and use TTYP to share how this extra information changes the pictures in our minds as we hear the story. Link what they have read and heard so far with Jeremy Strong's writing style.
- Hide the text and ask the children to use TTYP to take turns telling the story to each other taking one section at a time. You may wish to reveal the text a couple of times during this activity so that the children can refresh their memories.
- Ask the children to TTYP and use their knowledge of Jeremy Strong's style and fairy tales to make a prediction about the ending of the story. Take feedback.

Curriculum link: predicting from details stated and implied

Daily log – predicting PB

Purpose: for children to make a prediction about the story ending

- Ask the children to work in pairs and discuss the Predicting questions in the Pupils' Book p.36 and then write down their prediction for the story ending in their Daily log.

effective discussion; provide justifications for their views

Big Question CD

Purpose: for children to develop their skills of argument and discussion through a mini enquiry session based on a philosophical question relating to the work of the day

- Display the day's Big Question on the **CD (file 1.4)**:

  Is there ever any truth in a stereotype?

- Ask the children to TTYP to discuss. Collect feedback from partners and scribe some responses. Tell the children that each day's Big Question and their thoughts will be saved so that at the end of Week 2 they can then vote on which question to discuss more deeply. See Introduction for further notes (p.13).

DAY 2

explain and discuss their understanding of what they have read

Read a story version 3 A

Purpose: for children to hear and enjoy the full version of the story for the first time

- Tell the children they are now going to hear the whole story for the very first time. TOL about which parts you are looking forward to.
- Read the whole of *This Is NOT a Fairy Tale* from the Anthology pp.38–49 to the children with great enjoyment, and appropriate intonation. Make your storytelling a 'performance' and try to enhance Jeremy Strong's humour by using voices, etc.
- Make links to the predictions the children made in their Daily log and ask the children to TTYP to share their predictions and discuss how Jeremy Strong subverted the fairy tale construct in this story (turned it on its head). Take feedback.

identifying and discussing themes and conventions

Clarify CD

Purpose: for children to link the story to their understanding of Jeremy Strong's style

- Go through the story using TOL to identify some obvious examples of Jeremy Strong's style. Draw the children's attention to the knowing jokes about fairy tales, the subversion of stereotypes, the silly names, the mini episodes as Luke meets and surmounts each danger on the mountain and the way the main characters do not act as we might expect them to. Collect and write some examples of these key features under the headings on the **CD (file 2.1)**.
- You may wish to display the **CD (file 2.2)** and click 'TOL' for comments on Jeremy Strong's style.

Curriculum link: checking that the story makes sense to them

Think and link – map the story

Purpose: for children to understand the chronology and main points of the story

- Reveal the Story map on the **CD (file 2.3)** and TOL to discuss what the main events are. Draw the children's attention to the episodic nature of Luke's quest up the mountain and discuss the question mark at the end which represents the unknown aspect of the story, Ramona's ending.

Daily log

Purpose: for children to create a written or drawn representation of the story that can be used as an aide memoire

- Ask the children to map the story – you may wish to display the version on the **CD (file 2.3)** as a scaffold. Encourage them to add any particularly good 'Jeremy Strongisms'.

effective discussion; provide justifications for their views

Big Question

Purpose: for children to develop their skills of argument and discussion through a mini enquiry session based on a philosophical question relating to the work of the day

- Display today's Big Question on the **CD (file 2.4)**:

  What is the point of fairy tales?

- Follow the process as explained at the end of Day 1 (p.94).

DAY 3

exploring the meaning of words in context

Word power

Purpose: for children to visualise strong descriptive phrases and think about how they help the reader engage with a story

roamed ramshackle enthralled was as beautiful as the sunset launched flaming brands overcome

- Display the Power words on the **CD (file 3.1)**.
- Drag the phrases into the 'Focus' box and TOL describing the images and ideas these phrases bring to you as a reader. Make connections with the text as you do so, linking the phrases clearly with the images you are creating whilst reading.
- You may wish to print off the Power words from the **CD (file 3.2)** and display them on the Story wall.

checking that the story makes sense to them

Re-read a story version 3

Purpose: for children to gain a deeper understanding of the story and to see the text for the first time

- Let the children see and follow their own copy of the text in the Anthology pp.38–49 as you re-read the full version of the story aloud to them with enthusiasm, enjoyment and appropriate intonation. Place special emphasis upon the Power words in bold and stop at the Special phrases so that the children can 'jump in'. See Introduction for further explanation.
- Now ask the children to read their copy of the story with their partners, reading alternate sections each. Ask them to read together any words and phrases in bold with great expression. Explain that you will be listening in.

Curriculum link: identifying and discussing themes

Read and compare

Purpose: for children to compare and contrast the openings of stories by the same author

- Tell the children they are now going to look at the opening paragraphs of some of Jeremy Strong's books. Display these on the **CD (file 3.3)**.
- Print off the Key features of a Jeremy Strong story opening grid from the **CD (file 3.4)** for the children to complete.
- Read one of the openings aloud to the children and analyse it using TOL to complete the setting and main characters, any silly names, jokes or plays on words and the problem.
- Read another of the openings and ask the children to TTYP and do the same. Take feedback and add it to the chart on the **CD (file 3.5)**. Read the third opening to the children and ask them to TTYP and complete the grid.
- Then ask them to read the first two paragraphs of *This is NOT a Fairy Tale* in the Anthology p.38 and complete the grid either in pairs or independently.

discussing themes

Daily log

Purpose: for children to reflect on Jeremy Strong's writing style

- Tell the children to write three things that stand out to them about the three Jeremy Strong story openings they have read. Ask them to write down which opening made them want to read on most, and why.

effective discussion; provide justifications for their views

Big Question

Purpose: for children to develop their skills of argument and discussion through a mini enquiry session based on a philosophical question relating to the work of the day

- Display today's Big Question on the **CD (file 3.6)**:

  What's in a name?*

- Follow the process as explained at the end of Day 1 (p.94).

**This Big Question will be revisited on Day 11 – the first day of the Non-fiction week.*

DAY 4

Year 5 Grammar brackets, dashes and commas to indicate parenthesis

Grammar: parenthesis

Purpose: for children to understand the word 'parenthesis' and explore how it can be expressed with brackets, dashes and commas

- Display the **CD (file 4.1)**. Tell the children that you are going to read the beginning of the story This Is Not a Fairy Tale and you want them to listen carefully to see if they can hear any changes in the sound of your voice. Make sure that you give a significant pause at the dash and then say the subsequent words in a slightly lower tone of voice to emphasise the extra comment. If necessary, read it out twice.
- Take feedback. Explain that the dash showed you that you had to pause and that the next bit of text was slightly different to what had gone before because it was an extra comment. Explain that this extra bit of text is called 'parenthesis'.
- Click to the next slide use MT/YT to say the word 'parenthesis' and its definition. Explain that parenthesis is shown by dashes or brackets or even by commas, pointing out the examples on the slide.
- Click to the next slide and use MT/YT to read out the next extract, lowering your voice when reading out the text in brackets.
- Show the next slide and explain that in the story the writer needs to include some brackets in this extract, to show that one part could be said in a slightly different voice because it gave some extra information. Ask the children to TTYP to talk about where they would put the brackets to show parenthesis.

- Take feedback, trying out the children's suggestions, using your voice to emphasise where they put brackets. (The brackets should go round the sentence 'Behind the smile his teeth were firmly gritted.') Read out the text without the parenthesis, to show the children that it still makes sense, saying that this shows that parenthesis is 'extra' to the main text.
- Ask the children to look at the Grammar: parenthesis activity on p.36 of their Pupils' Book. Explain that they are going to take turns reading out some text, using their voices to show parenthesis, while their partner has to listen carefully (without looking at the text) and guess which part of the text is parenthesis. If necessary, remind them that parenthesis is shown by brackets, dashes or commas. Listen out for expressive, dramatic reading and share good examples with the whole class.

Homework Book p.14 provides further practice on parenthesis.

Curriculum link: checking that the story makes sense to them

Re-read a story version 3 A

Purpose: for children to deepen their understanding of a story by increasing familiarity with the text

- Ask the children to read the whole story silently from the Anthology pp.33–49. Tell the children that they can stop to record any thoughts, ideas, questions, and favourite bits in their Daily log as they read the text. Explain that it is more important for them to think about what they are reading than to finish first and, as they know the story, it doesn't matter if they don't finish this time.

compare characters

Drama – zoom in A

Purpose: for children to empathise with particular characters and to become familiar with a scenario that could be used later for writing

- Tell the children that you are going to focus on the mini episodes that form Luke's quest up the mountain to get to Princess Ramona.
- Ask the children to open the Anthology on p.42 and find the place where Luke comes across the flesh-tearing brambles.
- Read out the passage and ask the children to mime Luke's passage through the brambles using burning brands. (Explain the 'brands' are burning sticks, if necessary.)
- Next read Luke's encounter with the Waggletooth Witch starting with the witch saying "I'm going to put a nasty spell on you." (p.43)
- Ask the children to TTYP and discuss how this episode differs from the episode with the burning brambles. Take feedback.
- Explain how in the encounter with the Witch, Bear and Trolls Jeremy Strong uses dialogue to tell us what is happening, show us more about the characters and add humour.
- Ask the children to choose one of the three episodes with their partner, taking turns to be Luke or the Witch, Bear, etc. Give them time to read their episode a couple of times through and then ask them to act out the encounter without referring back to the text. Move around the room noting good examples of dialogue between the children and give feedback.

describing characters, integrating dialogue to convey character

Daily log

Purpose: for children to use dialogue when recalling an episode from the story

- Ask the children to use their ideas from the Drama session to write a short paragraph for the encounter they have acted out. Remind them to use dialogue.

Curriculum link: effective discussion; provide justifications for their views

Big Question (CD)

Purpose: for children to develop their skills of argument and discussion through a mini enquiry session based on a philosophical question relating to the work of the day

- Display today's Big Question on the **CD (file 4.2)**:

  Which are stronger, actions or words?

- Follow the process as explained at the end of Day 1 (p.94).

DAY 5

compare characters, discuss viewpoints

Who says? (CD) (PB)

Purpose: for children to develop their awareness of the narrative voice in a text

- Remind the children that the job of the narrator is to present the story in ways that the reader can understand. Display from where Luke meets Ramona to where he gives her the ultimatum in the story on the **CD (file 5.1)**. Ask the children to re-read it and then TTYP to identify: what *information* the narrator gives to the reader in this section.
- Collect feedback and scribe key points on the board.
- Tell the children that the narrator of the story is the 'voice' of the story. It can be jokey, solemn or even show strong likes and dislikes about the characters. It helps create the tone of the story. In this case the tone is funny and the narrator gives us all sorts of clues about how they feel about the characters and their actions.
- Tell the children that the narrator knows everything that has happened, where it has happened and can tell us all about the characters, but they weren't involved themself. Our narrator is a bit like a witness to events. Explain that this time, instead of looking at *what* the narrator is telling us, we are going to look at *how* they are telling us and what that might show us about their point of view. As the narrator is telling the reader the story they can show their point of view when they report what the characters say.
- Show the text again on the **CD (file 5.1)**. Click 'Highlights' to identify language that 'shows' the narrator's point of view of the characters.
- Ask the children to look at the Who says? sentences in the Pupils' Book p.37 and TTYP to discuss what the narrator thinks about Ramona and Luke. Collect feedback.
- Ask the children to consider how the narrator portrays Ramona and Luke. Ask: 'Do you think the narrator likes some characters more than others? How can you tell?'
- Ask for evidence to support their views. Encourage discussion, debate and opinions – not 'right' answers.

consider different accounts of the same event and discuss viewpoints

Drama – in role, Luke and Ramona

Purpose: for children to identify the dilemma faced by the main characters

- Focus the children on Ramona's dilemma: she is too scared to leave the castle but if she doesn't leave the castle Luke will go travelling the world without her.
- Use TOL to cover the main ideas: '*She has lived alone in the castle all her life, she wants to be rescued and can't imagine doing anything for herself, Luke isn't quite the Prince she expected to rescue her and she is too frightened to leave the castle and face the dangers on the way down even with Luke there to help her.*'
- Ask the children to TTYP and discuss Ramona's dilemma. Ask: 'How would she have to change in order to go down the mountain?' Take feedback.
- Now ask the children to think about Luke. 'Would he be able to persuade Ramona to leave with him?' Ask the children to TTYP and discuss how Luke could persuade Ramona to come down the mountain.

- Ask the children to work in pairs in role as Ramona and Luke. Tell them they are going to improvise Luke persuading Ramona to go with him and Ramona has to give reasons why she cannot go.

Curriculum link: drawing inferences and justifying with evidence, identifying key details that support ideas

What if not…? PB

Purpose: for children to consider how character, setting and plot each affect the other

- Ask the children to look at the What if not…? activity in the Pupils' Book p.37.
- TOL about the first What if not…? question with the children, modelling how you might explore how the story would change if Luke had been stupid like the other villagers: '*Perhaps he would have followed their advice and rubbed himself with acorn juice when he saw the Black Bear, which I think would have ended in disaster!*'

noting initial ideas

Daily log

Purpose: for children to keep a personal reading, writing and thinking log to record thoughts and ideas for their own writing

- Ask the children to record at least one more What if not…? question in their Daily log with some notes about how it would affect characters, plot or setting. For example: What if not *stupid*? What if the villagers had been *wise*? Think about how this would have affected Luke's desire to see the world. Suggest they use mind maps to help them record their ideas simply.

effective discussion; provide justifications for their views

Big Question CD

Purpose: for children to develop their skills of argument and discussion through a mini enquiry session based on a philosophical question relating to the work of the day

- Display today's Big Question on the **CD (file 5.2)**:

  Why does the unknown scare us?

- Follow the process as explained at the end of Day 1 (p.94).

WRITING FICTION

DAY 6

Build a sentence CD PB

pupils should understand, through being shown, the skills and processes essential for writing: that is, thinking aloud to generate ideas, drafting, and re-reading to check that the meaning is clear

Purpose: for children to compose dialogue that reveals information about a character and about what's happening

- Explain that you are going to look at the dialogue between Luke and the Black Bear. Look at the sentences on the **CD (file 6.1)**. Read them aloud and comment on how the author uses dialogue to reveal that the bear is gruff and possibly cross with the "Grrr", and that he tells us where Luke is ("halfway up this mountain") as well as why Luke is there ("to seek the hand of the Princess Ramona").
- Click "Next" to reveal the choices of words that could be used to show how the bear feels.
- Re-read sentence 1 using substitutions for "Grrr". Get feedback from the children about the different choices and comment on their effect on how the bear comes across.
- Remind the children how the dialogue is set out.
- Click "Next" again and repeat the activity for sentences 2 and 3 thinking about where Luke is and what he is doing there.

- Ask the children to TTYP and compose their own version of the final sentence (Luke's reply). Take feedback.

Modelled composition

- Tell the children that you will be composing a model of an episode of the story involving Ramona and her trip down the mountain. Say that the sentences that they have just been exploring are the inspiration for your episode.
- Now use modelled composition to write four sentences that will be used in the new story:

  "Arrggghh!" yelled Ramona with a high-pitched scream. "How did you suddenly appear, in these woods, in front of me?"

  "I crept up silently because I want to eat you," snickered the Giant Man-Eating Unicorn. "Are you a man?"

- Use TOL to explain what you are doing and orally rehearse and change each phrase before you write. Focus on the dialogue you choose to introduce Ramona and the Unicorn as they meet for the first time. Explain how you are setting up the tone of the meeting and following Jeremy Strong's style.
- Ask the children to say each sentence as you compose it using MT/YT and then write it on a flipchart or the board. Continue to use MT/YT as you TOL and model the writing process. N.B. A script of the writing process can be printed from the **CD (file 6.2)** if you want more support.
- Once you have finished modelling the writing process ask the children to read the full text in the Build a sentence activity in the Pupils' Book p.38.
- Hide your sentences. Ask the children, either individually or as partners, to compose their own sentence out loud using the sentence prompts in the Pupils' Book p.38. Do not let the children write in their Daily log until they can say their sentence out loud.
- Ask partners to take turns to develop each other's sentences. Encourage crossings out, switching words round, etc. Emphasise that this is writing in action – not a neat, finished piece of writing!

Tell a story (CD) (PB)

Purpose: for children to practise an oral retelling of a story

- Show the short text on the **CD (file 6.3)** that builds on the sentences from the last activity. This text builds on the encounter between Ramona and the Giant Man-Eating Unicorn.
- Read the text to the children.
- Explain that you are going to have a go at retelling this part of the story to them without looking at the written text. Retell the encounter between Ramona and the Giant Man-Eating Unicorn in your own words. Ask the children to listen carefully for:
  - missing information
  - additional information
  - more everyday language and less description
  - use of body language, facial expressions and funny voices to engage and amuse the audience, etc.
- Ask the children to TTYP to share what differences they noticed. They will need to refer to the written version of the text (Build a sentence) in the Pupils' Book p.38 after they have heard the retelling. Collect feedback.
- Now ask the children to take turns to read the text in Build a sentence in the Pupils' Book p.38 with expression and intonation.
- Next ask them to continue the story and try to develop the story orally with their partners using the sentence prompts in the Pupils' Book. They should swap

roles from teller to listener and vice versa when you say *stop and swap* at about 30 second intervals (two or three times), continuing the story from that point each time e.g. 'What should Ramona do?' Emphasis should be on building confidence in storytelling and keeping their audience engaged and interested!

Curriculum link: noting initial ideas

Daily log

Purpose: for children to start to generate ideas for their story

- Ask the children to write down one of the ideas they discussed with their partner for continuing the story.

effective discussion; provide justifications for their views

Big Question

Purpose: for children to develop their skills of argument and discussion through a mini enquiry session based on a philosophical question relating to the work of the day

- Display today's Big Question on the **CD (file 6.4)**:

  Is it the words you say that matter, or the way that you say them?

- Follow the process as explained at the end of Day 1 (p.94).

DAY 7

understand the processes essential for writing

Build an episode 1

Purpose: for children to be able to see a story grow through three stages of development

- Remind the children that they heard two versions of *This Is NOT a Fairy Tale* (Story version 1 and Story version 2) before they heard and read the full story. It prepared them to read the full story.
- Explain that you are going to show them two versions of a new episode to be written. These versions prepared you to write the full story. Show the questions on the **CD (file 7.1)** and explain that these were the questions that helped you to know what to put in this episode, which is Ramona's first mini episode as she travels down the mountain to Luke. TOL to explore the first question and then click 'Complete' to reveal the answer.
- Ask the children to TTYP to discuss the subsequent questions. Take feedback and then click 'Complete' to reveal the answers.
- Now display Build an episode 1 on the **CD (file 7.2)**.
- Read it out loud to the children. Explain that you are now going to show them another version of the new story to be written. This one has additional information and words – it has been developed.

Build an episode 2

Purpose: for children to be able to see a story grow through three stages of development

- Show Build an episode 2 on the **CD (file 7.3)**. TOL as you compare this version with Build an episode 1. Click 'Highlights' to show additional information, inclusion of jokes and dialogue. Note also the addition of past tense for Build and episode 2.

selecting the appropriate form, using similar writing as models for their own

Build an episode 3

Purpose: for children to see an example of writing that will provide a model for their own writing

- Explain to the children that you have tried to write in the style of Jeremy Strong in this episode. (The story has been provided as a model for writing.) Display the story on the **CD (file 7.4)**. Read the episode to the children.

- Now ask the children to take turns to read a section each of Build an episode 3 in the Pupils' Book pp.38–40. Using TTYP and oral feedback, ask the children to evaluate 'your' writing using the guide questions in the Pupils' Book p.40.

Curriculum link: noting ideas, provide reasoned justifications for their views

Daily log

Purpose: for children to keep a personal reading, writing and thinking log to record thoughts and ideas for their own writing

- Ask children to TTYP and share ideas for a title for the new episode of the story, which features Ramona. Ask them to record their best idea in their Daily log and explain why they think it is a good title.

effective discussion; provide justifications for their views

Big Question (CD)

Purpose: for children to develop their skills of argument and discussion through a mini enquiry session based on a philosophical question relating to the work of the day

- Display today's Big Question on the **CD (file 7.5)**:

  What would make you strong enough to face your greatest fear?

- Follow the process as explained at the end of Day 1 (p.94).

DAY 8

noting and developing initial ideas

Write a story 1 – plan (CD) (PB)

Purpose: for children to plan a new episode of Ramona's escape down the mountain

- Tell the children that they are going to write another episode of Ramona's escape down the mountain.
- Explain that you are going use a generic episode plan that shows Ramona meeting a scary character and using her wits to escape.
- Show the children the Write a story 1 – plan on the **CD (file 8.1)**.
- Ask the children to use the Blind date character summaries in the Write a story 1 – plan activity in the Pupils' Book p.41 to help them choose the character that Ramona will meet in their episode.
- Tell them to write their version of the plan in their Daily log using the information from the activity to help them.

considering how authors have developed characters, integrating dialogue to convey character and advance the action

Write a story 2 – dialogue (PB) (CD)

Purpose: for children to develop sentences and dialogue for their episode

- Use TOL to remind the children about the episode with the Giant Man-Eating Unicorn. TOL: *'First she was terrified and then she realised she had to try – she was clever, wasn't she? Ramona thought of a way to trick the Unicorn just like Luke.'*
- Ask the children to TTYP and to think about how Ramona might act when she meets the character they have chosen for their episode. Give the children time to talk about both their choices as they may have chosen different characters for their episodes.
- Ask the children to TTYP and to focus on how the two characters might talk to each other and remind them that talking in a story is called dialogue. Draw their attention to the dialogue in the unicorn episode (Build an episode 3) in the Pupils' Book p.39–40, (i.e. *"Are you the Giant Man-Eating Unicorn?" she asked with a quavering voice* to *"Thank you," said Ramona feeling very pleased with herself.*)
- Now ask the children to act in role as Ramona and the other character meeting in the forest. Tell them to concentrate on what the characters say and how they say it. Make sure that the children have time to take both roles so that they can practise their scenario.

- Look again at the bare bones of the episode Write a story 1 – plan on the **CD (file 8.1)**. Using TOL, and encouraging the children to offer their ideas, model how to develop sentence 1 by adding some information and phrases and changing some words.
- Repeat using sentence 2.
- Ask the children to develop sentence 3, the creature's dialogue, using the Write a story 2 – tips in the Pupils' Book p.42. Explain that you want them to compose individually the dialogue in their heads first. They must then make sure they can say it to their partner before they start to write.
- Now display this developed version of sentence 4 on the **CD (file 8.2)**:

  "Mmmm," murmured Ramona, "I don't think you are nasty at all. Actually, just between the two of us, I think you are gorgeous. A real beauty. Come here, I'm sure I have just the right ribbon to set off your eyes!"

- Guide children to identify features that show the development. Point out the parenthesis that has been included (just between the two of us).
- Ask the children to develop sentence 5 using the prompts in the Pupils' Book again and individually composing the dialogue in their heads first. They must then make sure they can say it to their partner before they start to write.

Curriculum link: conveying character

Daily log

Purpose: for children to keep a personal reading, writing and thinking log to record thoughts and ideas for their own writing

- Ask the children to think of something un-princessy for Ramona to do at the end of the episode to show her delight at escaping yet another mountain terror. Ask them to compose a couple of sentences to describe what she does in their Daily log.

effective discussion; provide justifications for their views

Big Question (CD)

Purpose: for children to develop their skills of argument and discussion through a mini enquiry session based on a philosophical question relating to the work of the day

- Display today's Big Question on the **CD (file 8.3)**:

  When can the weak be strong?

- Follow the process as explained at the end of Day 1 (p.94).

DAY 9

write by selecting appropriate grammar and vocabulary; describing settings, characters and atmosphere and integrating dialogue to convey character and advance the action

Write a story 3 (PB)

Purpose: for children to write their episode of Ramona's escape down the mountain

- Tell the children that they are ready to write their own episode of Ramona's escape down the mountain. Remind them of their 'bare bones' plan that sets out the structure of their episode.
- Ask them to use the Write a story 3 writing prompts in the Pupils' Book p.42 to guide them. Remind them to use any useful parts of their Daily log to help them.
- Remind them to look at the Story wall for Power words and phrases and a thesaurus for synonyms especially for the word 'said'.
- Encourage children to rehearse their opening sentence with their partners before they begin to write.
- You may wish to display the sentences you modelled with the children and/or the developed sentence 4.

DAY 10

Curriculum link: assessing the effectiveness of their own and others' writing

Share a story

Purpose: for children to read and share their episode of Ramona's escape down the mountain

- Ask the children to read through their own episode.
- Now tell them to re-read their episode and underline their favourite or best parts. Ask them to share these with their partners. Collect feedback on best bits from partners.
- Make sure that any powerful words or phrases are written on card and added to the Story wall.

Evaluate and edit (CD)

Purpose: for children to evaluate their own and their partner's work against specific criteria and then discuss how they could improve their work

- Display **CD (file 10.1)** to show the evaluation prompts and read them together using MT/YT.
- As a model, select an example of work from the children where the writing has met the criteria, and share this with the other children, explaining why it works well.
- Tell the children to take turns to read their partner's writing and discuss how well they have met the criteria.
- Ask children to discuss at least two changes they could make to improve their work following the partner discussion.

proofread for spelling and punctuation errors

Proofread

Purpose: for children to proofread their work and make changes to improve the accuracy of their grammar, punctuation and spelling

- Now ask the children to proofread their work. If you have noticed that several children need to improve on a particular aspect of spelling, grammar or punctuation, use this as a focus for the Proofread activity. Write an example which includes common errors from the children's writing and use this as a model.
- The children should always be checking for standard use of punctuation and correct spelling of common exception words.
- The following points would be relevant as the particular focus for this Unit:
  - checking that speech is punctuated correctly
  - correct use of brackets, dashes or commas to show parenthesis
  - checking the spelling of more ambitious vocabulary choices.

effective discussion; provide justifications for their views, distinguish between fact and opinion

Very Big Question (CD)

Purpose: for children to develop a willingness to broaden or revise their opinions through exploring one of the Big Questions in more depth

- See Unit 1 Day 10 for teaching notes on the Very Big Question (p.36).

Biography and autobiography

READING AND WRITING NON-FICTION

In the non-fiction part of the Unit children examine the difference between biography and autobiography initially linked to material about Jeremy Strong. They use material about the author Anthony Horowitz to practise note-taking and plan an author blurb for a book. They adapt this into a biographical presentation about him, using PowerPoint or another presentation tool.

See p.90 for the daily timetable for the Non-fiction week.

Non-fiction

Reading

Children will:

- decide what they would like to know about Jeremy Strong before they read his biography and autobiography
- explore how the biography and autobiography give different insights into Jeremy Strong's life
- discover how different types of biographical texts are organised to make it easy for readers to find information.

Writing

Key writing purpose to be shared with the children:

To write a short biography of Anthony Horowitz for the back cover of one of his books.

Writing evaluation to be shared with the children

My biography of Anthony Horowitz:

- uses information from the notes I made
- includes information that will interest readers of Anthony Horowitz's *Alex Rider* books
- uses organisational features to make the biography easy to follow and engage my reader's interest.

Grammar:

- includes adverbs and adverbials of time, so readers know when things happened.

See the Planning section of the Software ('Timetables' tab) for a printable version of the Writing purpose and evaluation.

DAY 11

Curriculum link: learn the conventions of different types of writing

Linking the texts (CD)

Purpose: for children to make links between the story text and the non-fiction text

- Display the Big Question from Day 3 on the **CD (file 3.6)**: *What's in a name?*
- Ask the children to TTYP and discuss how we find out about famous people like writers, actors, politicians, etc.
- Explain that biographical writing is a genre that is specifically about peoples' lives and examples of biographical writing include profiles in magazines, interviews, websites about a person, obituaries, CVs, biographies and autobiographies.

asking questions to improve their understanding

Introduction (CD) (A)

Purpose: for children to understand the context for the study of the non-fiction biography text

- Remind the children about the author they have been studying and recap some of the key features of his style: silly names, stereotypes turned upside down, mini episodes, jokes, characters acting unexpectedly.
- Ask the children to TTYP and discuss what they would like to find out about Jeremy Strong.
  N.B. These are not questions to ask Jeremy Strong himself but areas the class are keen to find information about.
- Take feedback and use it to create a mind map of questions, see **CD (file 11.1)**. Work with the children to group the questions into headings, for example: 'Jeremy Strong as a child', 'How Jeremy Strong writes', 'His books', 'His future books'.
- TOL to compose some class research questions using the headings as guidance: *'I can see that there are lots of questions about Jeremy at school so I'm going to write a question that asks how Jeremy's experiences at school helped him become a writer: How did school help Jeremy Strong become a writer?'*
- Ask the children to TTYP and compose a research question for the other headings in turn. Take feedback and compose a class list of research questions.
- Ask the children to read the biographical material about Jeremy Strong in the Anthology pp.50–51.
- After reading ask them to TTYP and find information in the text that answers the research questions the class came up with.

learn the conventions of different types of writing

Key features (A) (CD) (PB)

Purpose: for children to distinguish between biography and autobiography

- Tell the children that when a person writes about their own life it is called autobiography. Make a link between the prefix 'auto' and its meaning 'self' and show how the 'auto' is used in other words to change their meaning, e.g. autograph, automatic, autodestruct, automobile.
- Ask the children to read the autobiographical piece by Jeremy Strong from the Anthology pp.52–53.
- Use TOL to make comparisons between the two pieces of writing and tease out what is similar and different. For example: '*Both texts have the past tense for events that have happened, both have specific names and places. However, the autobiography uses the 1st person "I", and says things that only the writer can know, such as how he feels. The biography feels more factual and it can't say for sure what Jeremy Strong was thinking. It can't tell us what was inside his head. The autobiography is less strictly chronological, it is more an explanation of how he writes.*

- Display the Author information sorting activity on the **CD (file 11.2)**. Read each piece of information and initially decide which column it should go under: 'Biography', 'Autobiography' or 'Both'. Once you have sorted a few, ask the children to TTYP and decide where each piece of information belongs. Take feedback and continue to sort them.
- Ask the children to use the Key features comparison checklist in the Pupils' Book p.43 to identify examples of the key features in both of the text types with their partners. Take feedback and reiterate the examples that show how they are different.

Evaluating texts A

Purpose: for children to evaluate the usefulness of biography and autobiography as sources

- Remind the children of the class research questions. Model finding information that answers one of the questions in both of the texts. Use TOL to evaluate the type of information you gather from the two texts. For example: '*In the biography I can find out how many books Jeremy Strong writes and where he writes them, but in the autobiography it tells me how he writes them. The biography can give me facts but only the autobiography can give me Jeremy's point of view.*'
- Ask the children to re-read the two texts in the Anthology pp.50–53 and use TTYP to evaluate how they answer the class research questions. Take feedback about which text the children would use if they wanted to write about Jeremy Strong for the back pages of one of his books.

Curriculum link: noting ideas, drawing on reading and research

Daily log

Purpose: for children to keep a personal reading, writing and thinking log to record thoughts and ideas for their own writing

- Ask the children to collect biographical material about Jeremy Strong to add to the Jeremy Strong Book Corner – they could look for material at the back of his books, on his website, in the Reading Room on the Red House Books' website, on the Puffin website and on the CBBC website in the *Newsround* area.
- Tell them to choose one piece of information about Jeremy Strong and to write it along with where it came from in their Daily log.

DAY 12

using other similar writing as models for their own

Deconstruction 1 A CD

Purpose: for children to see an example of writing that will provide a model for the planning of their own writing

- Ask the children to find the Jeremy Strong biography text in the Anthology pp.50–51. Ask them to take turns to read a section of the biography aloud using expression and intonation.
- Display an excerpt of the text on the **CD (file 12.1)** and draw the children to the key features of a biography by using the highlight tool on your whiteboard to show:
  - past tense (describes what happened),
  - named person (Jeremy Strong in this case) or third person (he/she),
  - use of chronological order,
  - adverbials of time,
  - a formal tone or passive voice in parts
  - and accurate details including place names and names of people.
- Explain to the children that the Anthology text will be used as a reference to help them plan their own biography for the back of another author's book.

- Ask them to return to their copy of the text (in the Anthology) and ask them to TTYP to share whether the biography gives clear information on the following points:
  - Who the biography is about?
  - What got the author writing in the first place?
  - Important details such as date of birth, prizes won by the author
  - Interesting or unusual details to engage the reader
- Take feedback. Then return to the text in the Anthology to point out additional organisational features such as the text box with extra information and the pictures of Jeremy Strong.

Curriculum link: information retrieval

Read a biography

Purpose: for children to understand and locate examples of the key features of a biographical text

- Display the completed key features checklist grid on the **CD (file 12.2)** and explain the completed examples. Print out copies (one between two) of the empty grid from the **CD (file 12.3)**. Tell the children to work with their partners to complete their own grids using the whole text. Take feedback.

DAY 13

asking questions to improve their understanding

Deconstruction 2

Purpose: for children to compose the key questions that they want to answer in their biography

- Tell the children that they are going to be writing a biography about Anthony Horowitz for the back pages of one of his books (just like the materials at the back of the Jeremy Strong books). Explain that they are going to use a range of materials to help them gather information for this biography.
- Tell the children to look at the biographical source material about Anthony Horowitz in the Anthology pp.54–55. Guide them through the different types of material: timeline, information box of prize winning books, biographical information, etc.
- Remind the children of how they composed research questions to find out information about Jeremy Strong. Tell them that they are going to go through the same process for Anthony Horowitz so that they have a focus for their research.
- Ask the children to TTYP and discuss what they would like to find out about Anthony Horowitz. (N.B. these are not questions to ask Anthony Horowitz himself but areas the class are keen to find information about.)
- Take feedback and use it to create a mind map of questions, see **CD (file 13.1)**. Group the questions under headings, for example, questions about: 'Anthony Horowitz as a child', 'How Anthony Horowitz writes', 'His books', 'Future books'.
- TOL to compose a class research question using the headings as guidance. For example: '*There are lots of questions about the Alex Rider books. So a good research question could be "Where did Anthony Horowitz get the inspiration for the Alex Rider books?"*'
- Ask the children to TTYP and compose a research question for each of the other headings in turn.
- Take feedback and compose a class list of research questions. These will form the basis of their planning.

Curriculum link: summarising the main ideas

Build a biography – Top Tips for taking notes A PB

Purpose: for children to take notes from a range of sources and use these to make a plan

- Return to the biographical material about Anthony Horowitz in the Anthology pp.54–55 and model taking notes for one of the research questions.
- Show the children how notes are made up of key words and phrases and not whole copied chunks of text.
- Remind them how important it is to copy dates, names and other facts such as prize names correctly because they need to make their biography accurate.
- Show the children Top Tips for taking notes in the Pupils' Book p.44, which they can use to support them during the process.
- Ask the children to TTYP and discuss another one of the research questions. Take feedback and scribe notes.
- Then tell the children to TTYP and complete the note-taking process for their back page biography in their Daily log using the material in the Anthology.

Note-taking from video

- You may wish to give the children additional biographical material by giving them access to the Anthony Horowitz website: http://www.anthonyhorowitz.com
- There is also an opportunity to get autobiographical evidence for their writing if they read the *Blue Peter* interview which can be found at: http://www.bbc.co.uk/cbbc/articles/one-moment-with-anthony-horowitz

DAY 14

selecting the appropriate form and using other similar writing as models for their own

Deconstruction 3 A

Purpose: for children to see an example of writing that will provide an opportunity for them to evaluate the effectiveness of layout, organisation and clarity

- Tell the children to look at both of the biographies in the Anthology pp.50–51 and pp.54–55. Ask them to scan the texts looking at how the writer has helped the reader find information. Ask them to look out for: text boxes, pictures and captions, timelines, and headings and sub-headings.
- Tell the children that they will have limited space at the back of a book so they need to choose organisational features that group information together to help the reader.
- Ask the children to TTYP and discuss which of these organisational features would be good to have at the back of a book. Collect feedback.
- Look at some book jacket designs. Ask the children to TTYP and discuss how they are organised. Take feedback.
- Explain that these have a clear purpose and audience in mind. The audience is the intended reader and the purpose is to sell the book, other books by the same author and to make the author appear interesting or exciting.

using organisational and presentational devices to structure text and to guide the reader

Write a biography CD PB A

Purpose: for children to use their planning and notes to help them to write a biographical text

- Explain that you are going to show how a research question, and the notes collected to answer it, can be used to create a biography of Anthony Horowitz. Firstly you need to decide on a relevant area to research.
  TOL: *'For my biography, I'm going to write a paragraph about the Alex Rider books, because they are probably the best-known books written by Anthony Horowitz. So my question will be about these books.'*
- Display the example of a research question on the **CD (file 14.1)** and explain

that you have collected together some notes from the Anthology that give answers to this question (do not click 'Reveal' yet). Now you will make the notes into a paragraph.

- TOL: *'I will have three introductory sentences to tell the reader what they are going to read about*:
  "The Alex Rider books are probably Anthony Horowitz's best known works. There are eight of them and they tell the story of an ordinary 14-year-old who loses his parents and who is recruited, against his will, by MI6. But where did Anthony get his inspiration?" '
  TOL: *'I'm going to give basic information about the book. This is the question we are answering so I'm using it as the focus of the paragraph.*
  'I'm going to put the notes together in a couple of sentences to show how these experiences gave Anthony source material about mystery and secrets and a reason to write.'
- Click on 'Reveal' to display this part of the written paragraph. Tell the children that they can look at the complete paragraph in the Biography activity in the Pupils' Book p.45 if they wish.
- Tell the children that they are ready to write their biography of Anthony Horowitz for the back pages of one of his books using their research questions and notes. Remind the children that the information they use will have to fit onto a back page and will also need to include a picture of the author and images of some of the other books he has written. Explain that they will only have 200 words for their biography and its purpose is to interest children in the book and inform and excite the reader about the author, Anthony Horowitz.
- Tell the children they will need to focus on no more than three aspects of his life. Remind them to:
  - think about what they are going to focus on and how they are going organise it attractively
  - use the features checklist from Day 12 to help them
  - use any useful parts of their Daily log
  - look at the example texts in the Anthology pp.50–51 and pp.54–55 and the example biography in the Pupils' Book p.45
  - help the reader by organising your information using a logical chronology, progressing from Anthony's early life to the present.
- Encourage the children to rehearse their opening sentence with their partners before they begin to write.

DAY 15

Evaluate and edit (CD)

Purpose: for children to evaluate their own and their partner's work against specific criteria and then discuss how they could improve their work

Curriculum link: assessing the effectiveness of their own and others' writing

- Display **CD (file 15.1)** to show the evaluation prompts and read them together using MT/YT.
- As a model, select an example of a presentation where the children met the criteria, and share with the other children why it worked well.
- Tell the children to discuss with their partner how well they met the criteria.
- Ask children to discuss at least two changes they could make to improve their presentation following the partner discussion.

Curriculum link: proofread for spelling and punctuation errors

Proofread

Purpose: for children to proofread their work and make changes to improve the accuracy of their grammar, punctuation and spelling

- Now ask the children to proofread their work.
- If you have noticed that several children need to improve on a particular aspect of spelling, grammar or punctuation, use this as a focus for the Proofread activity. Write an example which includes common errors from the children's writing and use this as a model.
- The children should always be checking for standard use of punctuation and correct spelling of common exception words.
- The following points would be relevant as the particular focus for this Unit:
  - checking that capital letters have been used for proper nouns
  - checking the spelling of more ambitious vocabulary choices.

Fiction: Stories from another culture
Non-fiction: Non-chronological reports

Timetable

WEEK 1 Reading fiction *Dragon Slayer*

Day 1	Day 2	Day 3	Day 4	Day 5
The story store 🖶	Read a story version 3	Word power 🖶	Re-read a story version 3	Who says?
Read a story version 1	Clarify 🖶	Re-read a story version 3	Zoom in – character	Drama
Think and link	Think and link – Story volcano	Grammar: verb prefixes	Drama – role-play	Daily log
Read a story version 2	Daily log	Drama – forum theatre	What if not...?	Big Question
Daily log – predicting	Big Question	Daily log	Daily log	
Big Question		Big Question	Big Question	

WEEK 2 Writing fiction *Dragon Slayer*

Day 6	Day 7	Day 8	Day 9	Day 10
Build a sentence 🖶	Build an episode 1	Write a story 1*	Write a story 3	Share a story
Tell a story	Build an episode 2	Write a story 2		Evaluate and edit
Daily log	Build an episode 3 🖶	Daily log		Proofread
Big Question	Daily log	Big Question		Very Big Question
	Big Question			

*You will need a digital camera for this activity.

WEEK 3 Reading and writing non-fiction Non-chronological reports

Day 11	Day 12	Day 13	Day 14	Day 15
Linking the texts	Deconstruction 1	Deconstruction 2	Deconstruction 3	Evaluate and edit
Introduction	Grammar: suffixes	Build a non-chronological report	Write a non-chronological report	Proofread
Key features	Read a non-chronological report 🖶	Daily log		Create a podcast
Generic or specific?	Daily log			
Audience				
Daily log				

🖶: shows that a file should be printed out from the Software.

Overview of the Unit

This Unit explores story structure using a story from another culture. *Dragon Slayer*, which is an adventure story set in China, provides a very exciting model for the children to explore using pace and suspense to add excitement to their narratives.

The Non-fiction section of the Unit links to the *Dragon Slayer* story and introduces non-chronological reports through 'A field guide for ogre watchers'. For more information about the Non-fiction week and the Non-fiction writing evaluation criteria, see p.127.

The Homework Book provides a homework activity related to the content of this Unit for each of the three weeks.

Fiction

Reading

Children will:

- connect the story with their own experiences and previous reading
- understand the story's cultural and geographical context and use this to help to visualise the setting
- explore the obstacles that the main character has to overcome
- understand how a character's own self-image can differ from the perceptions of other characters and the reader.

Writing

Key writing purpose to be shared with the children:

To write a new adventure for Mai-Ling, using ideas from Dragon Slayer.

Writing evaluation to be shared with the children

My new episode:

- has an introduction, a build-up, a dilemma, suspense and a solution
- uses carefully-chosen language to describe Mai-Ling and her adventure to build in the reader's mind exactly the image I am thinking of
- includes some interesting details about Chinese customs, food or clothing so my reader can visualise the setting of the story.

Grammar:

- includes the first person and the past tense to show the reader I am writing from Mai-Ling's point of view
- includes adverbs and adverbials of time to create pace and drama, e.g. *Suddenly, In a flash.*

See the Planning section of the Software ('Timetables' tab) for a printable version of the Writing purpose and evaluation.

READING FICTION

Resources
- PB Pupils' Book, pp.46–55
- A Anthology, pp.56–69
- CD CD on interactive whiteboard, Unit 5
- GB Grammar Bank on CD
- HB Homework Book, pp.17–19

DAY 1

Curriculum link: increasing their familiarity with traditional stories from other cultures and traditions

The story store

Purpose: for children to understand the features of some stories from Chinese culture and contextualise the main themes

- Brainstorm any prior knowledge the children have of China, Chinese stories and Chinese culture. They may have more cinematic than text-based references so you may need to make links to the main religion of China (Buddhism), traditional dress and food to create a starting point. Collect these on the mind map on the **CD (file 1.1)**.
- Display the two stories on the **CD (file 1.3)** and read them aloud to the children. Make it plain that these are ancient stories like our myths and legends and represent different parts of Chinese culture. Ask the children to TTYP (Turn to your partner) and discuss their first impressions of the stories. Take feedback sensitively, approaching any sweeping generalisations about Chinese culture.
- Model using one of the texts to find evidence about Chinese culture. TOL (Think out loud), highlighting any appropriate phrases. For example in the first story you can find out about religion, belief in magic, Chinese food and the Chinese feudal system.
- Ask the children to TTYP and discuss the remaining two stories (you can print the summaries from **CD [file 1.2]**), gathering as much evidence about Chinese culture as they can. Take feedback and where appropriate add any information to the mind map.

Read a story version 1

read a story from another culture

Before the lesson, you may wish to watch the video demonstrating Read a story version 1 (with a Year 5 story). This can be found in the Extras section of the software.

Purpose: for children to become familiar with Story version 1; the bare bones of Dragon Slayer

- Read Story version 1 aloud to the children all the way through. Do not read the numbers aloud. Do not reveal the ending.

  Story version 1

  1. A dragon shattered the peace of the people in a tiny village in China by settling on the rim of a nearby ancient volcano.
  2. The worried villagers sought advice from their village Wise Man who told them not to worry.
  3. The dragon came to the village but left the villagers unharmed and the villagers praised the Wise Man's advice.
  4. Then the dragon came and took the villagers' livestock.
  5. The villagers sought advice from their village Wise Man who told them not to worry.
  6. The dragon took one child and then another…
  7. The villagers demanded that something be done.
  8. The Wise Man devised a way of choosing a villager to slay the dragon.
  9. A young girl was chosen. She was afraid and didn't know how to slay a dragon.
  10. She went up the mountain and met a mysterious stranger on the way, who gave her advice.
  11. She carried on up the volcano determined to rid the village of the dragon. But how?
- Use MT/YT (My turn/Your turn) and TTYP for each point – you will need to break down the longer points. Use exaggerated intonation and emphasis to make the sentences memorable. This will help the children to 'hold' the basic story in their heads. Then display Story 1 on the **CD (file 1.4)** for the children to read.

Curriculum link: making comparisons

Think and link

Purpose: for children to make links and connections to the landscape of China and the setting of the story

- Display the Chinese setting images on the **CD (file 1.5)** and make a link between the image of the volcano and the ancient volcano that features in Story version 1. Use the image as a stimulus for discussion about the setting of the story. Ask the children to TTYP and imagine what it would be like for Mai-ling to climb the extinct volcano. Take feedback and record some of the ideas.
- Look at the other setting pictures and ask the children to select a good setting for the *Dragon King* story. Ask the children to TTYP and discuss why they have chosen a particular setting. Take feedback. Do the same for the *Kitchen God* story.
- Look at the remaining setting and ask the children to TTYP and discuss what type of story the setting evokes for them.

predicting; identifying how language, structure, and presentation contribute to meaning

Read a story version 2

Purpose: for children to examine how Story version 2 provides additional information for the reader and for children to become more familiar with the story before they hear the full version

- Read Story version 2 aloud to the children.

  Story version 2

  1. A great emerald-green dragon shattered the peace of the people in the tiny village of Yishan in China by settling on the rim of a nearby ancient extinct volcano
  2. The worried villagers sought advice from their village Wise Man, Yen, who pondered the problem and gathered the villagers by ringing the ceremonial bell and told them not to worry because dragons loved gold and jewels and the villagers did not have any.
  3. One day the dragon swooped over the village and breathed red and orange flames. The villagers cowered but the dragon flew off. The villagers praised Yen for his wisdom.
  4. Then the dragon came back in the night and stole a goat and then it came by day and swooped to steal more.
  5. The villagers, afraid that they would starve, sought advice from Yen who told them that the dragon would soon tire of the livestock and go away.
  6. Then one awful day the dragon took a child and then another…
  7. The villagers demanded from Yen that something should be done but none of them wanted to kill the dragon.
  8. So the Wise Man said that whoever chose the green pebble from his bag would be sent to slay the dragon.
  9. Mai-ling, a twelve-year-old girl, was chosen. She quaked with fear because she didn't know how to slay a dragon.
  10. She left the village, sobbing, to go up the mountain and met a mysterious black and white robed stranger on the way, who gave her advice and a silver dagger.
  11. She carried on up the volcano, clutching the silver dagger, determined to rid the village of the dragon. But how?

- Now display Story version 2 on the **CD (file 1.6)**. Click 'Highlights' to highlight additional information and information which helps to show the setting and context for the story.
- TOL and use TTYP to share how this extra information changes the pictures in our minds as we hear the story. Link what they have read and heard so far with the other Chinese stories. Are there any similarities about customs, clothes and settings?

- Hide the text and ask the children to use TTYP to take turns telling the story to each other taking one section at a time.
- Ask the children to TTYP and make a prediction about the ending of the story. Take feedback.

Curriculum link: predicting from details stated and implied

Daily log – predicting

Purpose: for children to make a prediction about the story ending

- Ask the children to work in pairs and discuss the Predicting questions about the story so far in the Pupils' Book p.46 and then write their prediction for the story ending in their Daily log.

effective discussion; provide justifications for their views

Big Question

Purpose: for children to develop their skills of argument and discussion through a mini enquiry session based on a philosophical question relating to the work of the day

- Display today's Big Question on the **CD (file 1.7)**:

  What can other cultures teach us?

- Ask the children to TTYP to discuss. Collect feedback from partners and scribe some responses. Tell the children that each day's Big Question and their thoughts will be collected on the CD and saved so that at the end of Week 2 they can then vote on which question to discuss more deeply. See Introduction for further notes (p.13).

DAY 2

explain and discuss their understanding of what they have read

Read a story version 3

Purpose: for children to hear and enjoy the full version of the story for the first time

- Tell the children that they are now going to hear the whole story for the very first time. TOL about which parts *you* are looking forward to.
- Read the full story of *Dragon Slayer* from the Anthology pp.56–63 to the children with great enjoyment, and appropriate intonation. Make your storytelling a 'performance' and try to add to the suspense of how Mai-ling is going to slay the dragon.
- Make links to the predictions the children made in their Daily log and ask the children to TTYP to share their predictions and discuss how Mai-ling managed to slay the dragon.

increasing their familiarity with traditional stories from other cultures and traditions

Clarify

Purpose: for children to link Dragon Slayer *to their understanding of Chinese customs and attitudes explored in other stories*

- Before you start this activity print off the Culture and customs grid from the **CD (file 2.1)** for the children to complete and the stories in the Story store from the **CD (file 2.2)** for the children to use during this activity. Do not give these out to the children yet.
- Go through the *Dragon Slayer* story in the Anthology pp.56–63 using TOL to identify some obvious signifiers and examples of Chinese customs. Some TOL prompts are included on the **CD (file 2.3)** to help you.
- Now model using the grid on the **CD (file 2.4)** with *The Origin of the Kitchen God* story. Click 'Complete' to display the completed column entries for this story one click at a time.
- Now give out the printouts of **CD (files 2.1 and 2.2)** and ask the children to TTYP and complete the grid for *The Dragon King's Daughter.* The answers for the other two stories are included as a model.

Curriculum link: summarising the main ideas

Think and link – Story volcano PB

Purpose: for children to understand the chronology and main points of the story

- Go through the Think and link Story volcano in the Pupils' Book p.47 using TOL to discuss the questions. Make sure the children know what the main events are. Draw the children's attention to the mysterious stranger's part in the story and to how Yen changes.

Daily log PB

Purpose: for children to create a written or drawn representation of the story that can be used as an aide memoire

- Ask the children to use the Think and link Story volcano in the Pupils' Book p.47 to help them create their own plan of the story in their Daily log using the questions to help them. Encourage them to add any cultural details that will enrich the story.

effective discussion; provide justifications for their views

Big Question CD

Purpose: for children to develop their skills of argument and discussion through a mini enquiry session based on a philosophical question relating to the work of the day

- Display today's Big Question on the **CD (file 2.5)**:

  Are leaders always wise?

- Follow the process as explained at the end of Day 1 (p.116).

DAY 3

exploring the meaning of words in context

Word power CD

Purpose: for children to visualise strong descriptive phrases about the setting of the story

ancient extinct darkened beneath the shadow crept beam nestling bed rattled

- Display the Power words on the **CD (file 3.1)**.
- Drag the phrases into the 'Focus' box and TOL describing the images and the ideas these phrases about the setting bring to you as a reader. Make connections with the text as you do so, linking the phrases clearly with the images you are creating whilst reading.
  For example: '*The phrase "the foothills of an ancient extinct volcano" makes me think of a high lush place. I imagine looking up from the foothills to a distant peak and, although I know the volcano is extinct and that it won't erupt, it makes me feel uneasy. The word "ancient" makes me think that this story is also old and that the volcano might hold secrets.*'
- You may wish to print off these words from **CD (file 3.2)** to display on your Story wall.

checking the story makes sense to them

Re-read a story version 3 A

Purpose: for children to gain a deeper understanding of the story and to see the text for the first time

- Let the children see and follow their own copy of the text in their Anthology pp.56–63 as you re-read the full version of the story aloud to them with enthusiasm, enjoyment and appropriate intonation. Place special emphasis upon the Power words in bold, stopping so that the children can 'jump in'. See Introduction for further explanation.

- Now ask the children to read their copy of the story with their partners, reading alternate sections each. Ask them to read together any words and phrases in bold with great expression. Explain that you will be listening in.

Curriculum link: Year 5 Grammar
verb prefixes

Grammar: verb prefixes (CD) HB

Purpose: for children to identify and understand the meaning of a range of common verb prefixes

- Remind the children that a prefix is a group of letters that are added to the front of a word to change its meaning. Tell them that they are going to look at prefixes that are added to verbs to make new verbs. (If necessary, remind them that verbs describe what someone or something is doing, e.g. *read, think, play.*)
- Display the **CD (file 3.3)** and read out the extract. Then use MT/YT to re-read the final sentence, *More and more disappeared and the people complained loudly.*
- Tell the children that there are two verbs in this sentence. Ask them to TTYP to decide which words are the verbs. Take feedback, then click 'Highlights' to show the words *disappeared* and *complained.*
- Say that one of these verbs uses a common prefix, *dis-*. Ask the children to TTYP to select the right verb and then as a class they should say the word, chorally – *disappear.*
- Click to the next slide to show the meaning of the prefix *dis-*. Use MT/YT to read out the meaning. Then look at the example word 'disagree'. Click 'Hide/Reveal' to cover the prefix and show just the word 'agree', then click 'Hide/Reveal' again to show the 'dis- ' and show the complete word that now means the opposite of the root word 'agree'.
- Read out the next example and ask the children to TTYP to talk about what it means. Take feedback, then continue with the other examples, ensuring the children understand how the prefix *dis-* alters the meaning of each root word to give the opposite sense.
- Click to the next slides, and follow the same procedure with the prefixes *mis-* and *re-*.

Homework Book p.17 provides further practice on verb prefixes.

Drama – forum theatre (CD)

Purpose: for children to investigate how the setting affects how a character acts

- Explain that you are going to set up a piece of 'forum theatre'. This is when an audience is shown a shortish play in which a central character encounters an obstacle which they are unable to overcome. In this case the action will be Mai-ling creeping up upon the dragon and the obstacle will be that she does not know how to slay it. At this point the audience can give the character advice and the play is re-run but if a member of the audience feels that the main character might usefully have tried a different strategy, they can stop the action, take the character's place, and try out their idea.
- You will need two 'actors' to portray the dragon and Mai-ling and you will need to agree a sign to stop the action during the forum theatre performance.
- Ask the actors to act out Mai-ling climbing over the edge of the volcano rim and seeing the sleeping dragon. Freeze the action at this point and ask the children to TTYP to discuss their ideas about how Mai-ling could slay the dragon. Take feedback and re-run the action using the audience participation to change the action as they see fit.

- Now show the children one of the alternative settings (lake, snowy mountainous village, swamp) on the **CD (file 3.4)** and ask the actors to act out the scene as before. Does it work in the same way? Use forum theatre to discuss how the action should change and re-run the action using the audience participation to change the action as they see fit.

Curriculum link: describing settings

Daily log (CD)

Purpose: *for children to investigate how a change of setting would influence how a character acts*

- Show the children one of the remaining settings on the **CD (file 3.4)** and ask them to write a short paragraph in their Daily log showing how Mai-ling would defeat the dragon in that setting. Remind the children of the how Power words created clear images of the setting in the reader's mind and encourage them to use some of their own in this paragraph.

effective discussion; provide justifications for their views

Big Question (CD)

Purpose: *for children to develop their skills of argument and discussion through a mini enquiry session based on a philosophical question relating to the work of the day*

- Display today's Big Question on the **CD (file 3.5)**:

  What makes a community work?

- Follow the process as explained at the end of Day 1 (p.116).

DAY 4

read silently, checking that the book makes sense to them

Re-read a story version 3 (A)

Purpose: *for children to deepen their understanding of a story by increasing familiarity with the text*

- Ask the children to read their copy of the whole story silently in the Anthology pp.56–63. Tell the children that they can stop to record any thoughts, ideas, questions and favourite bits in their Daily log as they read the text. Explain that it is more important for them to think about what they are reading than to finish first and, as they know the story, it doesn't matter if they don't finish this time.

drawing inferences and justifying these with evidence from the text

Zoom in – character (CD) (A)

Purpose: *for children to use inference and deduction to gather information about Yen from the text*

- Ask the children to TTYP and discuss all that they know about the village Elder, Yen. Take feedback and add information to the mind map on the **CD (file 4.1)**.
- Model how to TOL, using the Anthology text to make inferences about Yen. For example: '*It says here, "They crowded into the meeting hall where Yen stood." I can infer from this that Yen knows he is important and respected because the villagers crowd into the hall, eager to hear his advice.*'
- Ask the children to TTYP and use the text to make an inference about Yen. Take feedback and add the inferences to the mind map.
- Model making a deduction about how Yen thinks using the text. For example, TOL: '*I think when Yen uses the black bag and the green stone to choose someone to slay the dragon he is being deceitful. He does not have an answer to the problem of the dragon and all his pondering and stroking of his beard is just an act to appear wise. I think Yen hoped the problem of the dragon would just go away.*'
- Ask the children to TTYP and make a deduction about Yen's character through his actions. Take feedback noting any further ideas onto the mind map.

Curriculum link: asking questions to improve their understanding

Drama – role-play (CD)

Purpose: for children to write questions to elicit more information about a character (Mai-ling)

- Display the Helping hand on the **CD (file 4.2)** and tell the children that you are going to demonstrate composing some 'open questions' to ask Mai-ling to find out more about, her. Explain that an open question can be answered in many ways, it isn't just a 'yes' or 'no' question. It could reveal how Mai-ling feels or the reasons for her actions or it could just give some detail about where she lives or her problem.
- TOL to compose your question. First pin down the area you want to find out about for example:

  'I would like to know about how Mai-ling felt as she left the village to climb the volcano. I don't want to say "Did you feel worried?" because she could just say "yes" or "no". So I need to start my question with "How". "How did you feel as you walked away from the village?"'
- Ask the children to TTYP to create other questions they'd like to ask Mai-ling. Tell them to record three questions in their Daily log. Take feedback and create a list of class questions.
- Now tell the children that they need to take notes in their Daily log as you act in role as Mai-ling to answer the questions. At the end of the session take feedback about what the children found out during the role-play.

drawing inferences and justifying with evidence, identifying key details that support ideas

What if not…? (PB)

Purpose: for children to consider how character, setting and plot affect each other

- Ask the children to look at the What if not…? questions in the Pupils' Book p.48. Model the first What if not…? and TOL about how the story would change if Yen had been wise and told the villagers that he didn't know what to do about a dragon: *'Perhaps they could have worked as a community together, the livestock might not have been taken and they certainly would have done something before the dragon did something awful like eat a child. Perhaps the villagers could have tried to communicate with the dragon?'*
- Ask children to TTYP and discuss this and the other What if not…? questions. Collect feedback and encourage others to build upon the argument. Give your opinion too.

Daily log

Purpose: for children to keep a personal reading, writing and thinking log to record thoughts and ideas for their own writing

- Ask the children to record at least one more What if not…? in their Daily log with some notes about how it would affect characters, plot or setting. For example: What if not *Mai-ling*? What if *Yen* had gone up the volcano? Suggest they use mind maps to help them record their ideas simply.

effective discussion; provide justifications for their views

Big Question (CD)

Purpose: for children to develop their skills of argument and discussion through a mini enquiry session based on a philosophical question relating to the work of the day

- Display today's Big Question on the **CD (file 4.3):**

  Which is worse: doing nothing or acting rashly?
- Follow the process as explained at the end of Day 1 (p.116).

DAY 5

Curriculum link: compare characters

Who says? A PB

Purpose: for children to develop their awareness of the narrative voice in a text

- Remind the children that the job of the narrator is to present the story in ways that the reader can understand.
- Remind the children of how the narrator portrays Yen. Draw their attention to how in the story he repeatedly ponders the problem for days and strokes his long grey beard to look wise. The narrator does not see Yen as a man of action. The narrator uses their words to make a judgement about the character.
- Ask the children to TTYP and scan the text to look for other examples of the narrator giving a negative impression of Yen.
- Tell the children that this narrator knows everything that has happened, where it has happened and can tell us all about the characters, but they weren't involved themself. Our narrator is a bit like a witness to events. However a narrator also has a point of view about the characters.
- Ask the children to look at the Who says? sentences in the Pupils' Book p.48 and TTYP to discuss what the narrator thinks about Yen, Mai-ling and the dragon. Collect feedback. Ask: 'Do you think the narrator likes some characters more than others? How can you tell?'
- Ask for evidence to support their views. Encourage discussion, debate and opinions – not 'right' answers.

Drama

Purpose: for children to see how the status of characters affects the story

- Organise the children into groups of four. Tell them to share out the roles of Yen, Mai-ling, a villager and the mysterious stranger. Explain to them that they are going to act out the story but you are going to freeze-frame the action from time to time.
- When you tell the children to freeze they are going to say what status they feel they have at that point in the story, 1 being very low and 4 being on top of the world. Ask the children to check that their body language mirrors the status they feel and change the freeze-frame accordingly.
- Stop the story at several points and ask the children to reflect on whether their status has changed. Yen and Mai-ling should almost swap status by the end of the story.
- Come together and ask children to TTYP to reflect on how Yen loses his status and how the villagers' status subtlety changes with Mai-ling as the village elder. Take feedback.

summarising the main ideas

Daily log

Purpose: for children to reflect upon the status change of one character through the story

- Ask the children to choose either Yen or Mai-ling and reflect upon how their status changes as the story progresses by mapping these changes onto their Story volcano from Day 2 using numbers to represent the changes in her status.

effective discussion; provide justifications for their views

Big Question CD

Purpose: for children to develop their skills of argument and discussion through a mini enquiry session based on a philosophical question relating to the work of the day

- Display today's Big Question on the **CD (file 5.1)**:

  What can we learn from difficult times?

- Follow the process as explained at the end of Day 1 (p.116).

WRITING FICTION

DAY 6

Curriculum link: understand, through being shown, the skills and processes essential for writing: that is, thinking aloud to generate ideas, drafting, and re-reading to check that the meaning is clear

Build a sentence

Purpose: for children to compose a description that reveals information about a character and creates an atmosphere

- Reveal the description of the sleeping dragon on the **CD (file 6.1)**. Read it aloud and comment on how the author uses incredibly precise description to give an atmospheric description of the dragon asleep.
- Draw the children's attention to the phrase 'veined wings' and help the children imagine the thin leathery muscular veiny-ness of the wings. Make sure that the children understand the word 'lustre' and if they are unsure explain that lustre is a shine or gloss.
- Click on the **CD (file 6.2)** and reveal the choices of words that could be used as synonyms for descriptions of the dragon.
- Re-read sentence 1 using substitutions for 'emerald green'. Take feedback from the children about the different choices and comment on their effect.
- Repeat the activity for sentences 2 and 3.
- Ask the children to TTYP and compose their own version of the final sentence. Take feedback.

Modelled composition

- Tell the children that you will be composing a model of an episode of the story involving Mai-ling and the ogre.
- Now use modelled composition to write the first few sentences of the new episode.
- Use TOL to explain what you are doing and orally rehearse and change each phrase before you write.
- Ask the children to say each sentence as you compose it using MT/YT and then write it on a flipchart or the board. Continue to use MT/YT as you now TOL and model the *writing* process. N.B. A script of the writing process is on the **CD (file 6.3)** and can be printed if you want more support.
- Hide your sentences. Now ask the children, either individually or as partners, to compose their own sentences out loud using the Build a sentence prompts in the Pupils' Book p.49. Do not let the children write in their Daily log until they can say their sentences aloud.
- Ask partners to take turns to develop each other's sentences. Encourage crossings out, switching words round, etc. Emphasise that this is writing in action – it is not a neat, finished piece of writing!

Tell a story

Purpose: for children to practise an oral retelling of a story

- Read the Tell a story short text in the Pupils' Book p.49 that builds on the sentences from the last activity. This text builds on the encounter between Mai-ling and the ogre.
- Explain that you are going to have a go at retelling this part of the story to them without looking at the written text (prepare your oral retelling before the lesson). Ask them to listen and look carefully for:
  - missing information
  - additional information
  - more everyday language and less description
  - use of body language, facial expressions and funny voices to engage and amuse the audience, etc.

- Ask the children to TTYP to share what differences they noticed. They might wish to refer to the written version of the text in the Pupils' Book after they have heard the retelling. Collect feedback.
- Tell the children that they are going continue to develop the story orally with their partners. They should swap roles from teller to listener and vice versa when you say *stop and swap* at about 30 second intervals (two or three times), continuing the story from that point each time. What should Mai-ling do? Emphasis should be on building confidence in storytelling and keeping their audience engaged and interested!

Curriculum link: noting initial ideas

Daily log

Purpose: for children to start to generate ideas for their story

- Ask the children to write down one of the ideas they discussed with their partner for continuing the story.

effective discussion; provide justifications for their views

Big Question (CD)

Purpose: for children to develop their skills of argument and discussion through a mini enquiry session based on a philosophical question relating to the work of the day

- Display today's Big Question on the **CD (file 6.4)**:

  What makes a monster monstrous?

- Follow the process as explained at the end of Day 1 (p.116).

DAY 7

plan writing by noting and developing ideas; consider how authors have developed characters and settings

Build an episode 1 (CD)

Purpose: for children to be able to see a story grow through three stages of development

- Remind the children that they heard two versions of *Dragon Slayer* (Story versions 1 and 2) before they heard and read the full story. It *prepared* them to *read* the full story.
- Explain that you are going to show them two versions of a new episode to be written which is about Mai-ling investigating the ogre troubling her village. These versions *prepared* the writer to *write* the full story. Tell the children that this episode is going to be written in the first person from Mai-ling's point of view.
- Show the questions on the **CD (file 7.1)** and explain that these were the questions that helped the writer (writing in role as Mai-ling) know what to put in this episode, which is about Mai-ling gathering evidence about the ogre that threatens her village before she decides what to do. Click 'Complete' to reveal Mai-ling's answers.
- Display Build an episode 1 on the **CD (file 7.2)**. Read it aloud to the children. Link the story to the questions Mai-ling answered. Explain that you are now going to show them another version of the new story to be written. This one has additional information and words – it has been developed.

Build an episode 2 (CD)

Purpose: for children to be able to see a story grow through three stages of development

- Show Build an episode 2 on the **CD (file 7.3)**. TOL as you compare this version with Build an episode 1. Click 'Highlights' to highlight examples of the use of the past tense, additional information and the inclusion of description. Use the highlighter tool on your whiteboard to highlight Mai-ling's feelings and point of view.

Curriculum link: using other similar writing as models for their own

Build an episode 3

Purpose: for children to see an example of writing that will provide a model for their own writing

- An example story is provided as a model for writing. Take the role of the writer of this story during these activities.
- Display the story on the **CD (file 7.4)**. Explain that you were trying to write a continuation of the original story and were taking into account the Chinese cultural ideas you have examined as well as telling the story through Mai-ling's eyes, and were writing in the past tense and first person. Read the episode to the children.
- Print off copies of the story from the **CD (file 7.5)**. Ask the children to take turns to read the story using expression and intonation. Using TTYP and oral feedback, ask the children to evaluate the story using the guide questions.

noting ideas, provide reasoned justifications for their views

Daily log

Purpose: for children to keep a personal reading, writing and thinking log to record thoughts and ideas for their own writing

- Ask the children to TTYP and discuss ideas for a sub-heading for the new section of the story. Ask them to record their best idea in their Daily log and explain why they think it is a good title.

effective discussion; provide justifications for their views

Big Question

Purpose: for children to develop their skills of argument and discussion through a mini enquiry session based on a philosophical question relating to the work of the day

- Display today's Big Question on the **CD (file 7.6)**:

  What does 'know your enemy' mean?*

- Follow the process as explained at the end of Day 1 (p.116).

**This Big Question will be revisited on Day 11 – the first day of the Non-fiction week.*

DAY 8

plan their writing, noting and developing initial ideas

Write a story 1

Purpose: for children to plan a new episode describing how Mai-ling will defeat the ogre

- Organise the children into small groups of four and ask them to work together to create four freeze-frames (see Introduction) to represent the story of Mai-ling investigating the ogre. Ask some of the children to show their freeze-frames and feed back focusing on describing the action that the freeze-frames represent.
- Show the abridged Story volcano on the **CD (file 8.1)** and use it to discuss the structure of the ogre investigation episode.
- Now ask the children to TTYP and discuss how Mai-ling and the villagers might defeat the ogre. Remind them of the ogre's weaknesses, its slowness and noisiness. Once it has eaten it falls into a deep sleep. Take feedback and create a class mind map of ways that the ogre might be defeated.
- Now ask the children to work in their groups and improvise Mai-ling and the villagers defeating the ogre using one of the strategies they devised. Ask the children to think of four freeze-frames that sum up the main points of their story. Take digital photos of each of these to use later.
- Return to the Story volcano on the **CD (file 8.1)** and map out a plan of the story using one set of the freeze-frame pictures as the example. Make notes on the story volcano and draw the children's attention to the points where the action is at its most tense.
- Now ask the children to use the Story volcano in the Write a story 1 activity in the Pupils' Book p.50 and their freeze-frame photos to plan their story.

Curriculum link: creating atmosphere

Write a story 2 (CD)

Purpose: for children to develop different sentence types for their episode

- Display the extracts of the model text from the **CD (file 8.2)**. Click 'TOL' to reveal each TOL think bubble.
- After the first TOL ask the children to TTYP and discuss how they might use the sentence types to describe Mai-ling coming upon the ogre a second time, focusing on building up an atmosphere of destruction, pace and zooming in on detail. Give the children time to compose four sentences orally and then write them in their Daily log.
- After the second TOL ask the children to TTYP to use their story plan and discuss how they imagine Mai-ling's confrontation with the ogre. Ask them to orally compose some sentences, which cause tension, suspense and pace and then when they are confident note them down in their Daily log.

plan their writing

Daily log

Purpose: for children to keep a personal reading, writing and thinking log to record thoughts and ideas for their own writing

- Ask the children to zoom in on the part of their story where Mai-ling confronts the ogre. Tell them to run the scene like a film in their heads and then when they have all the details ask them to closely plan that part of the story. They may wish to draw a diagram of the action, an annotated picture of the setting, a mind map or a storyboard.

effective discussion; provide justifications for their views

Big Question (CD)

Purpose: for children to develop their skills of argument and discussion through a mini enquiry session based on a philosophical question relating to the work of the day

- Display today's Big Question on the **CD (file 8.3)**:

  Is it true that many heads are better than one?

- Follow the process as explained at the end of Day 1 (p.116).

DAY 9

describing settings, characters and atmosphere

Write a story 3 (PB)

Purpose: for children to write their episode of Mai-ling's defeat of the ogre

- Tell the children that they are ready to write their own episode of Mai-ling's defeat of the ogre. Remind them of their pictures and Story volcano plans that set out the structure of their episode. Draw their attention to the importance of their episode maintaining the feeling of a Chinese story. Say their episode should be written from Mai-ling's point of view, as if they are Mai-ling (in the first person) and in the past tense.
- Ask them to use the composition prompts in the Write a story 3 activity in the Pupils' Book p.51 to guide them. Remind them to use any useful parts of their Daily log to help them.
- Remind them to look at the Story wall for Power words and phrases, and a thesaurus for synonyms especially for the words they use to describe the ogre's strength and size.
- Encourage children to rehearse their opening sentence with their partners before they begin to write.

- Remind the children of how you developed the description of the ogre as well as the different sentence types that you explored in the last session that create atmosphere, tension and pace. You may wish to display the developed sentence 4 from Day 6 on the CD.

DAY 10

Curriculum link: assessing the effectiveness of their own and others' writing

Share a story

Purpose: for children to read and share their episode of Mai-ling's defeat of the ogre

- Ask the children to read through their own episode.
- Now tell them to re-read their episode and underline their favourite or best parts. Ask them to share these with their partners. Collect feedback on best bits from partners.
- Make sure that any powerful words or phrases are written on card and added to the Story wall.

Evaluate and edit (CD)

Purpose: for children to evaluate their own and their partner's work against specific criteria and then discuss how they could improve their work

- Display **CD (file 10.1)** to show the evaluation prompts and read them together using MT/YT.
- As a model, select an example of work from the children where the writing has met the criteria, and share this with the other children, explaining why it works well.
- Tell the children to take turns to read their partner's writing and discuss how well they have met the criteria.
- Ask children to discuss at least two changes they could make to improve their work following the partner discussion.

proofread for spelling and punctuation errors

Proofread

Purpose: for children to proofread their work and make changes to improve the accuracy of their grammar, punctuation and spelling

- Now ask the children to proofread their work. If you have noticed that several children need to improve on a particular aspect of spelling, grammar or punctuation, use this as a focus for the Proofread activity. Write an example which includes common errors from the children's writing and use this as a model.
- The children should always be checking for standard use of punctuation and correct spelling of common exception words.
- The following points would be relevant as the particular focus for this Unit:
  - checking spelling of words and phrases used to move time on, e.g. *suddenly, at that moment , in a flash, instantly*
  - checking verb prefixes have been used correctly, if included
  - checking that a variety of sentence lengths and structures have been used.

effective discussion; provide justifications for their views, distinguish between fact and opinion

Very Big Question (CD)

Purpose: for children to develop a willingness to broaden or revise their opinions through exploring one of the Big Questions in more depth

- See Unit 1 Day 10 for teaching notes on the Very Big Question (p.36).

Non-chronological reports

READING AND WRITING NON-FICTION

The non-fiction part of the Unit links to *Dragon Slayer* and introduces non-chronological reports through 'A field guide for ogre watchers'. Children explore the text type further by reading and deconstructing texts about the kraken and mythical dragons. They gather information about different dragons and then write their own field guide.

See p.112 for the daily timetable for the Non-fiction week.

Non-fiction

Reading

Children will:

- read non-chronological texts to find out more information about ogres
- identify the key features of non-chronological texts and look at how they are structured to help the reader find information
- understand how non-chronological texts can be altered to suit different audiences and purposes

Writing

Key writing purpose to be shared with the children:

To write a clearly-structured non-chronological report about a species of dragon.

Writing evaluation to be shared with the children

My non-chronological report:

- includes facts and information from my notes that will engage and inform the reader
- lays out information with organisational features that make it easy for my reader to find the information they want, e.g. *subheadings, diagrams* and *fact boxes*
- includes detail that I think the reader will find interesting.

Grammar:

- is written in the third person and the present tense
- includes adverbs and adverbials that show why things happen, e.g. *This is useful because… However… Therefore…* to signpost cause and effect for my reader.

See the Planning section of the Software ('Timetables' tab) for a printable version of the Writing purpose and evaluation.

DAY 11

Curriculum link: learn the conventions of different types of writing

Linking the texts

Purpose: for children to make links between the story text and the non-fiction text

- Display the Big Question from Day 7 on the **CD (file 7.6)**: *What does 'know your enemy' mean?*
- Ask the children to TTYP and discuss how and where we can go to find information about a topic. Take feedback and make a point of asking the children to consider the reliability of the sources they are suggesting.
- Remind the children how Mai-ling went to study the ogre before she made a plan for how to defeat it. Explain that Mai-ling would have benefited from a book that described the ogre, its habits, habitat and other useful information. This kind of information is often found in a non-chronological report because this text type describes the way things are.

Introduction

Purpose: for children to understand the context for the study of the non-fiction text

- Tell the children that they are going to work together to decide what information would help Mai-ling identify the type of ogre she has in her forest. She needs a short concise guide to help her. It should have all the information she needs to track and defeat the ogre.
- Fill in the Ogre mind map on the **CD (file 11.1)**, reviewing the facts that Mai-ling found out about the ogre (see **CD file 7.1**). Ask the children to TTYP and discuss what other information would be good to know about the ogre. Take feedback and write key words on the mind map to summarise the areas the children would like to find out more about.
- Look at the mind map and TOL to explain how the children can group the information under larger headings. For example you could group together key words that relate to the ogre's size, strength and what it looks like under the heading 'Appearance of ogres'.
- Ask the children to TTYP and think of headings to group the different information on the mind map. Take feedback and together come up with a list of headings which could include: 'Ogre's behaviour', 'Ogre's preferred habitat', 'Ogre's diet', 'Interesting or unusual ogre facts'.
- Explain to the children that it would really help Mai-ling if she had some pictures and diagrams to help her easily understand all the information. Ask the children to TTYP and discuss what type of pictures and diagrams might be useful for Mai-ling.
- Tell the children that Mai-ling has composed a short non-chronological report for other people suffering from ogre attacks called 'A field guide for ogre watchers'. Ask them to read it in the Pupils' Book pp.52–53 and TTYP to discuss how the information is organised.

learn the conventions of different types of writing, exploring the meaning of words in context

Key features

Purpose: for children to understand and be able to identify the terms 'causal language' and 'generic', which are key features of a non-chronological text

topic headings descriptive language causal language generic subject third person present tense

this is useful because however therefore this is because which are… so that

- Ask the children to re-read 'A field guide for ogre watchers' in the Pupils' Book pp.52–53 and tell them this is a non-chronological report text. Explain that a field guide is a guide to tracking or hunting ogres 'in the field', i.e. their natural outdoor habitat.
- Display the checklist on the **CD (file 11.2)** and allude to it whilst talking through the 'Field guide for ogre watchers.' Note the features of non-chronological reports that are used, e.g.
  - She has grouped the information under topic headings written as questions.
  - She has used descriptive language to accurately describe ogre behaviour, habitat and physical appearance.
  - She has used causal language to make connections between ideas (*which means, or*).
  - She has written generically about ogres and people – she does not mention ogres or people by their names.
  - She has used the third person present tense (*ogres are very aggressive*).
- Display the Special phrases material on the **CD (file 11.3)** which looks more closely at causal language.
- Click on the words to reveal them in context.
- Explain the meaning of the word or phrase before revealing it in the sentences. Use MT/YT to get the children to practise using the causal words and phrases in the example sentences.

Generic or specific? PB

Purpose: *for children to understand the difference between generic and specific*

- Remind the children that Mai-ling wrote her field guide about ogres in general. This is called the generic – she does not call the ogre by its name but talks about ogres generally. She could talk about a type of ogre and still be talking generally, for example a Chinese mountain ogre, but if she started to talk about Fred the ogre she would be using the specific.
- Ask the children to do the Generic or specific? activity in the Pupils' Book p.53. Support the children by doing the first three for them.

Curriculum link: identifying the audience for writing, selecting the appropriate form

Audience PB

Purpose: *for children to recognise that the basic structure of non-chronological texts will change to suit different audiences and purposes*

- Refer the children again to 'A field guide for ogre watchers' in the Pupils' Book pp.52–53 and tell them that it is short but contains all the information an ogre watcher might need. It is concise.
- Tell the children to TTYP and discuss how Mai-ling has tailored her information to be useful for an ogre hunter. (*It is short, detailed, there are Top Tips and there are images.*)

describing characters

Daily log

Purpose: *for children to keep a personal reading, writing and thinking log to record thoughts and ideas for their own writing*

- Ask the children to think about the ogre. Why might it behave as it does? Imagine seeing the world through its eyes. Ask them to write a short paragraph describing its progress through the forest, eating the deer and snacking on the squirrel.

DAY 12

Curriculum link: using similar writing as models for their own

Deconstruction 1

Purpose: for children to see an example of writing that will provide a model for the planning of their own writing

- Ask the children to find 'The Kraken' text in the Anthology pp.64–66. Explain that it is a non-chronological report and ask them to take turns to read a section aloud using expression and intonation.
- Display an excerpt of the text on the **CD (file 12.1)** and draw the children's attention to the key features of a non-chronological report by using the highlighter tool on your whiteboard to highlight: third person, present tense, that it is non-chronological (not in time order), technical language, the use of the generic not specific (*squid, scientists, fishermen*), descriptive language to create precise and accurate descriptions, and causal language (*this is because, therefore, however, so*).
- Explain to the children that this text will be used as a reference to help them to plan their own non-chronological report, which will be about another mythical creature. Ask them to return to their copy of the text in the Anthology pp.64–66 and to TTYP to share whether the non-chronological report gives clear information about the points listed on the **CD (file 12.2)**.
- Take feedback. Then return to 'The Kraken' in the Anthology to point out additional organisational features such as the timeline, the pictures with captions and the short factual sentences organised by bullet points.

Year 5 Grammar converting nouns and adjectives into verbs using suffixes

Grammar: suffixes

Purpose: for children to understand that nouns and adjectives can be changed into verbs, by adding suffixes to the root word.

- Remind the children that suffixes are a group of letters that are added to the end of a word to change its meaning or make it into a different word class, for example suffixes can change nouns and adjectives into verbs.
- Display **CD (file 12.3)** to show three suffixes. Explain that these three common suffixes can turn nouns and adjectives into verbs. Read out the suffixes using MT/YT. Click 'Next' and read the example. Click 'TOL' to show a TOL bubble and use it to explain how the verb is formed by adding a suffix.
- Click through the rest of the slides and read through the examples, using the TOL bubble to explain how the verbs are formed by adding suffixes. Use MY/TY to read through the extracts showing the verbs within a sentence. Note that these extracts are all from the Kraken text in the Anthology.
- Ask the children to look at the Grammar: suffixes activity on p.53 of their Pupils' Book. Use MT/YT to read through the words, checking comprehension. Then tell the children to complete the activity orally and then write the pairs of words in two columns, headed 'noun or adjective' and 'verb'. Take feedback, ensuring the children understand the role of the suffixes.

Homework Book p.19 provides further practice on suffixes.

learn the conventions of different types of writing

Read a non-chronological report

Purpose: for children to understand and locate examples of the key features of a text

- Display the Key features of a non-chronological report checklist on the **CD (file 12.4)**.
- Click 'Complete' to show the examples. Refer to the text in the Anthology as you explain the completed examples.

- Tell the children to work with their partners to complete their own grids. They can be printed from the **CD (file 12.5)** for children to write on to record their answers.
- Collect answers and use the completed grid on the CD to clarify points and show different examples.

Curriculum link: retrieve and record information from non-fiction

Daily log

Purpose: for children to keep a personal reading, writing and thinking log in order to record thoughts and ideas for their own writing

- Ask the children to note down three fabulous facts that they found out about the kraken or squid.

DAY 13

asking questions to improve their understanding

Deconstruction 2

Purpose: for children to compose the key questions that they want to answer in their non-chronological report

- Tell the children that they are going to produce a class 'Field guide for dragon spotters'. The field guide will give information useful to someone who needs to prepare for dragon spotting as well as being concise enough to use in the field.
- Remind the children of the type of information they found in the kraken and ogre non-chronological reports in the Anthology. Ask them to TTYP and discuss what type of information would be useful to a dragon spotter. Make sure they understand that they are composing topic headings similar to those they composed for Mai-ling's ogre field guide. Headings should include: 'Diet', 'Behaviour', 'Appearance', 'Habitat', 'Extra information'.
- Use the mind map on the **CD (file 13.1)** to collect their feedback (remember to save this).
- Ask the children to return to 'A field guide for ogre watchers' and 'The Kraken' texts to discuss any diagrams, pictures or other visual information that they think might help a dragon spotter.

noting and developing initial ideas, drawing on reading and research

Build a non-chronological report

Purpose: for children to take notes from a range of sources and use these to make a plan

- Tell the children that information about dragons comes from many sources. Books such as *Dragonology* and the Internet are good places to start.
- Explain that this material gives us a vast amount of knowledge about dragons and that you are going to model taking information about a specific dragon: the Knucker.
- Display your annotated mind map on the **CD (file 13.1)** whilst the children read the 'Knucker dragon' text in the Build a non-chronological report activity in the Pupils' Book p.54.
- Ask the children to TTYP and discuss any information they found that can go under any of the sub-headings on the mind map.
- Now display the Knucker mind map on the **CD (file 13.2)** and TOL as you reveal the notes (by clicking 'Complete') taken from the 'Knucker dragon' text.
- Leave the final sub-heading 'Habitat' blank (do not click 'Complete' for this) and ask the children to TTYP and use their Daily log to take their own notes for this sub-heading. Take feedback and reveal the notes on the CD if you wish.
- Display the Dragon map of the world on the **CD (file 13.3)** and ask the children to decide which dragon they would like to investigate further using books and the Internet.

- Some children may wish to use the information about the Knucker in the Pupils' Book p.54 as one of their sources.
- Tell the children to use the source material available to them and to take notes from their Daily log to complete a mind map.
- You may wish to use an extra session for note-taking and research. A good general video source about dragon tracks and signs is www.ologyworld.com.

Curriculum link: noting ideas

Daily log

Purpose: for children to keep a personal reading, writing and thinking log to record thoughts and ideas for their own writing

- Ask the children to think of a good title for their entry in the field guide and write it in their Daily log.

DAY 14

selecting the appropriate form and using other similar writing as models for their own

Deconstruction 3 A

Purpose: for children to see an example of writing and for them to evaluate the effectiveness of layout, organisation and clarity

- Tell the children to look at 'The Kraken' and 'A Dragon Spotter's Guide to the Chinese Lung Dragon' in the Anthology pp.67–69. Ask them to scan the texts looking at how the writer has helped the reader find information. Ask them to look out for: text boxes, pictures and captions, timelines, headings and sub-headings, diagrams, maps and Top Tips.
- Tell the children that they will have limited space in their field guide and it needs to be easy for the reader to find information quickly. The reader will need visual references and Top Tips to help them if they get into a sticky situation. So they need to set out their text clearly using organisational features that make it very easy to read.
- Ask the children to TTYP and discuss which of these organisational features would be good to use in their field guides. Collect feedback.

understand, through being shown, the skills and processes essential for writing

Write a non-chronological report PB

Purpose: for children to use their planning and notes to help them to write a non-chronological text

- Tell the children that you are going to model turning one set of notes, on 'Behaviour' on your spidergram into a short warning for dragon spotters. TOL: *'I'm going to create a warning for dragon spotters. I want to make sure that anyone in the field is wearing adequate clothing. So I'm going to focus on how the Knucker spits venom.*

  'I must write in the third person and present tense and I'm not going to use specifics. I shall write in the generic using "dragon spotters" and "Knucker" as my nouns. I shall use descriptive language to describe the protective clothing properly so a dragon spotter will put the right equipment on.'
- Use this text as your model:

  The Knucker: A warning for dragon spotters!

  Unlike most dragons the Knucker does not breathe fire, rather it spits a toxic acid venom. This venom has the power to liquidise living matter. Dragon spotters should therefore protect themselves by wearing heavy lead-lined clothing and protective goggles, whenever Knucker watching.
- Tell the children to read the text in the Write a non-chronological report activity in the Pupils' Book p.55 before they start their own dragon text.

- Tell the children that they now have all the information they need to write an entry in the field guide about *their* dragon.
- Direct them to the Key features of a non-chronological report checklist in the Pupils' Book p.55.

DAY 15

Curriculum link: assessing the effectiveness of their own and others' writing

Evaluate and edit (CD)

Purpose: for children to evaluate their own and their partner's work against specific criteria and then discuss how they could improve their work

- Display **CD (file 15.1)** to show the evaluation prompts and read them together using MT/YT.
- As a model, select an example of work from the children where the writing has met the criteria, and share this with the other children, explaining why it works well.
- Tell the children to take turns to read their partner's writing and discuss how well they have met the criteria.
- Ask children to discuss at least two changes they could make to improve their work following the partner discussion.

proofread for spelling and punctuation errors

Proofread

Purpose: for children to proofread their work and make changes to improve the accuracy of their grammar, punctuation and spelling

- Now ask the children to proofread their work. If you have noticed that several children need to improve on a particular aspect of spelling, grammar or punctuation, use this as a focus for the Proofread activity. Write an example which includes common errors from the children's writing and use this as a model.
- The children should always be checking for standard use of punctuation and correct spelling of common exception words.
- The following points would be relevant as the particular focus for this Unit:
  - checking spelling of more ambitious vocabulary choices
  - checking that capital letters have been used for proper nouns.

perform their own compositions, using appropriate intonation, volume, and movement so that meaning is clear

Create a podcast

Purpose: for children to create a podcast

- Now tell the children that they are each going to rewrite their non-chronological report. They are going to choose one of the dragons they have written about and create a one-minute podcast for other dragon spotters explaining everything about it. Tell them to think carefully about:
  - what aspect of the dragon information they want to focus on
  - making the information exciting and clear for their target audience
  - any changes that would improve the text that came up in the evaluation exercise and scoring
  - which images and key words would best support their podcast
  - how they are going to work as a group to present their podcast.
- These prompts can displayed on **CD (file 15.2)**.
- Once the children have completed and presented their podcasts, take feedback and comment on how successful they were.

Unit 6

Fiction: Dramatic conventions (playscripts)
Non-fiction: Discussion texts

Timetable

WEEK 1 Reading fiction *Father's Day*

Day 1	Day 2	Day 3	Day 4	Day 5
The script store	Script version 3	Re-read a script version 3	What if not...? 🖶	The script store
Conventions of form	Word power 2 🖶	Think and link 1 🖶	Role on the wall 🖶	Dramatic improvisation
Read a script version 1	Read a script version 3	What's explicit, what's implicit?	Formal/informal?	Daily log
Read a script version 2	Daily log	Daily log	Daily log	Big Question
Word power 1 🖶	Big Question	Big Question	Big Question	
Daily log				
Big Question				

WEEK 2 Writing fiction *Father's Day*

Day 6	Day 7	Day 8	Day 9	Day 10
Build a character	Build a script 1	Evaluation 🖶	Write a script 3	Share a script
Show, don't tell	Build a script 2	Write a script 1		Evaluate and edit
Build a speech	Build a script 3	Write a script 2		Proofread
Daily log	Daily log	Daily log		Very Big Question
Big Question	Big Question	Big Question		

WEEK 3 Reading and writing non-fiction Discussion texts

Day 11	Day 12	Day 13	Day 14	Day 15
Introduction	Deconstruction 1	Write a discussion 1	Deconstruction 2	Write a discussion 3
Word power 🖶	Grammar: commas	Role-play 2	Write a discussion 2 🖶	Summarise
Balance and bias 🖶	Role-play 1	Daily log	Daily log	Evaluate and edit
Personal and impersonal	Daily log			Proofread
Daily log				

🖶: shows that a file should be printed out from the Software.

Overview of the Unit

In Weeks 1 and 2 of this Unit children study a playscript, *Father's Day*, about step-sibling rivalry. The writer, Lou Kuenzler, uses a range of dramatic conventions to show subtleties of character and the conflicting emotions experienced within families. Children study the plot and sub-plot and dramatic convention. Elements of performance are also included. The children look at the stages of development of a script, then go on to write an extra scene for the play.

Other script forms, such as broadcast scripts on non-fiction themes, will also be explored in this Unit. Discussion texts are studied, looking at the conventions of oral debate. For more information about the Non-fiction week and the Non-fiction writing evaluation criteria, see p.150.

The Homework Book provides a homework activity related to the content of this Unit for each of the three weeks.

Fiction

Reading

Children will:

- explore characters' motivations and thoughts using implicit and explicit information from *Father's Day*
- explore the importance of specific characters and moments
- understand that scripts are written for different purposes and have different degrees of formality.

Writing

Key writing purpose to be shared with the children:

To create a new scene for a play about a bully, using dialogue and stage directions to develop a clear picture of the characters' feelings and actions.

Writing evaluation to be shared with the children

My new scene:

- uses playscript conventions, e.g. *names before speech, stage directions* and *scene descriptions*
- *shows* what the characters are thinking and feeling through their actions
- builds characters that are interesting and convincing for the readers, by thinking carefully about how they should speak.

Grammar:

- includes formal or informal dialogue for the characters depending on the situation, e.g. *more formal for the policeman, less formal for the children.*

See the Planning section of the Software ('Timetables' tab) for a printable version of the Writing purpose and evaluation.

Fiction: Dramatic conventions (playscripts)

Father's Day by Lou Kuenzler

READING FICTION

Resources

PB Pupils' Book, pp.56–64

A Anthology, pp.70–80

CD CD on interactive whiteboard, Unit 6

GB Grammar Bank on CD

HB Homework Book, pp.20–23

DAY 1

Curriculum link: learn the conventions of different types of writing

The script store (CD)

Purpose: for children to develop an awareness of different types of scripts and their purpose

- Explain that a script is any text intended for use by a performer. For example, a script could be: a *fiction* stage play or film or a *non-fiction* broadcast such as a documentary, news item or advert.
- Use the **CD (file 1.1)** to show extracts from different types of scripts. Explain that they are all scripts about unusually high winds that caused a tree to crash to the ground. Read them to the children, identifying them as non-fiction scripted broadcasts and a fiction script.
- Tell the children that the newsreader in script A, the reporter in script B, and the presenter in script C are all reading from prepared scripts to give the audience facts and information. These are non-fiction scripts about the storm.
- Explain that the actors in script D are also reading from a script but they are pretending to be someone else – they are acting and giving a dramatic performance to entertain the audience. This is a fiction script based on the storm.
- Explain that they are going to look more closely at playscripts.

Conventions of form (CD)

Purpose: for children to revise the conventions of the form of a playscript

- Remind the children that there are rules about the layout of scripts so that everyone involved in the play knows what to say, and what to do. Click on the **CD (file 1.2)**. Use the speech bubbles to explain the basic features and conventions of scripts.
- Explain that in a full script there would also be a list of the characters.
- Tell the children they are now going to hear the 'bare bones' of a full playscript about a family and we are going to call it Script version 1.

read plays

Read a script version 1 (CD)

Purpose: for children to become familiar with Script version 1, the bare bones of the script, Father's Day

- Read Script version 1 aloud to the children all the way through. Do not read the numbers aloud. Do not reveal any surprises or the ending of the final play and do not read the numbers aloud. Use MT/YT (My turn/Your turn), TTYP (Turn to your partner) for each point. Use exaggerated intonation and emphasis where appropriate. This is to help the children to 'hold' the basic script in their heads.

Script version 1

Characters

- A boy
- A girl
- Girl's mum
- Boy's dad

Scene 1

A Saturday morning.

Action

1. A boy and a girl are arguing.
2. Each tries to get Mum on their side.
3. Mum tells the audience about the family situation.
4. Dad arrives on the scene.

Scene 2

Later on

Action

5. Mum reminds the children about Father's Day.
6. The children share a joke but it turns into an argument.
7. The girl talks about the Father's Day present she is going to buy.

Scene 3

Late afternoon

Action

8. The boy's actions make the girl angry and upset.

Scene 4

Father's Day

Action

9. An unexpected twist is shown.
10. Father's Day could be a success or a disaster.

- Display Script version 1 on the **CD (file 1.3)** for the children to read.

Curriculum link: identifying how language, structure, and presentation contribute to meaning

Read a script version 2 (CD)

Purpose: for children to examine how Script version 2 provides additional information for the reader and for them to become more familiar with the script before they hear the full version

- Tell the children that they are now going to hear a fuller version of the script that will tell them more about the characters and the action.
- Read Script version 2 (below) out loud with appropriate enthusiasm and intonation.

Script Version 2

Characters

- Cameron – a boy
- Ria – a girl
- Lorraine – Ria's mum
- Steve – Cameron's dad

Scene 1

A Saturday morning in June in the kitchen.

Action

1. Cameron and Ria rush into the kitchen.
2. They are squabbling about taking turns on the computer.
3. They tell tales on each other to try to get Lorraine on their side.
4. Lorraine informs the audience about the complicated step-family circumstances.
5. Steve arrives on the scene and makes jokes to calm things down.

Scene 2

Later the same day in the kitchen.

Action

6. Lorraine reminds the children that tomorrow is Father's Day.
7. She tells them that they should buy Steve a present.
8. The children share a joke and Ria is pleased that Cameron is being nice.
9. But it turns into a heated argument about their relationships with Steve.
10. Ria chatters about the perfect Father's Day gift she intends to buy for Steve, her step-father.

Scene 3

Late afternoon in the kitchen.

Action

11. Ria is crying and shouting at Cameron because of something he has done.
12. They start quarrelling about Cameron's actions but it becomes a bitter row about other things.

Scene 4

Father's Day. Steve is opening his presents.

Action

13. Steve explains to the audience how he sees the step-family situation.
14. A surprising turn of events is revealed and we see how people can change and develop.
15. After all the bickering, Father's Day could be a triumph or a complete disaster.

- Now display this version on the **CD (file 1.4)**. Click 'Highlights' to identify the additional information:
  - we now know characters' names – *Ria, Cameron, Lorraine and Steve*
  - addition of the fact that the children are *squabbling about taking turns on the computer*
  - addition of the information that it is a *step-family with complicated circumstances*
  - we now know that Steve uses *jokes* and humour to deal with family tensions
  - addition of the adjective *heated* to describe the second argument
  - we now know that the arguments are not just about computers and presents but about *other things*
  - additional information that the *twist or turn in events* leads to *change*.
- TOL (Think out loud) and use TTYP to share how this extra information changes the pictures in our minds, our thoughts and ideas about the characters and events as we hear the script.

Curriculum link: exploring the meaning of words in context

Word power 1

Purpose: for children to increase their knowledge of and application of synonyms and to examine how writers use language for effect

quarrelling arguing bickering squabbling unexpected twist surprising turn of events success triumph

- Tell the children that there are some words in Script version 2 that mean the same as 'arguing' in Script version 1. Tell them that these synonyms can show different types of arguing. 'Bickering' appears on the second screen but is not highlighted – ask children if they can spot another word for 'arguing' on the second screen.
- Display the extracts from Script version 1 and 2 on the **CD (file 1.5)** and then click 'Synonyms' to identify the synonyms.

- Repeat the procedure for *unexpected twist* and the synonymous phrase *surprising turn of events* and then the word *success* and synonym *triumph* in Script version 2
- TOL and use TTYP to share an example of how these words change the pictures in our minds as we hear the scripts.
- Print all of these words and phrases from the **CD (file 1.6)** and display on your Playscript wall.

Curriculum link: predicting what might happen from details stated and implied

Daily log

Purpose: for children to keep a personal reading, writing and thinking log to record thoughts and ideas for their own writing

- See notes on Daily log in Unit 1 (p.24). Explain that they are going to continue to collect thoughts and ideas in their Daily log.
- Ask the children to TTYP to discuss what they think Cameron might have done (sentence 11 in Script version 2) to make Ria so upset and angry that she is 'crying and shouting at him'. Ask them to record one or two ideas about what Cameron's actions might have been.

effective discussion; provide justifications for their views

Big Question

Purpose: for children to develop their skills of argument and discussion through a mini enquiry session based on a philosophical question relating to the work of the day

- Display today's Big Question on the **CD (file 1.7)**:

  Are friends just as important as family?

- Ask the children to TTYP to discuss. Collect feedback from partners and scribe some responses. Tell the children that each day's Big Question and their thoughts will be put in a safe place until the end of Week 2. They will then vote on which question to discuss more deeply. See Introduction for further notes (p.13).

DAY 2

explain and discuss their understanding of what they have read

Script version 3

Purpose: for children to hear and enjoy the full version of the script for the first time

- Tell the children that they are now going to hear the whole script for the first time. Show your enthusiasm before you start. TOL about which parts you can't wait to hear about, etc.
- Open **CD (file 2.1)** to hear the playscript read by actors.
- Ask the children to follow the script in the Anthology pp.70–78 as it is read by actors.
- At the end of the play, ask the children to TTYP to discuss the Script version 3 questions in the Pupils' Book p.56. Then collect feedback.

exploring the meaning of words in context

Word power 2

Purpose: for children to learn the meaning of rare vocabulary and discuss how these words and phrases are used in this script

malicious *eccentricities* *quaint* *devious* *iridescent*

- Before the lesson, print all of these words and their synonyms from the **CD (file 2.2)** and display on your Playscript wall.
- Look at the words and their definitions in the Pupils' Book p.56 with the children and then read the sentences to them. Ask the children to repeat the sentences using MT/YT, giving dramatic emphasis and actions as you say them.

- Tell the children that most of the words spoken by the characters is everyday spoken language but there are some words that are not commonly used in everyday conversations.
- The children must hear, see and repeat the word in your teaching and conversation throughout the day: "I'm sure you didn't mean to be malicious!"
- Encourage them to use the words at home with friends and family so that they become embedded in the children's own spoken (and eventually, written) vocabulary.
- Now ask the children to do the Word power 2 activity in the Pupils' Book p.56.

Curriculum link: checking that the script makes sense to them

Read a script version 3 (CD) A

Purpose: for children to gain a deeper understanding of the script

- Let the children follow their own copy of the text in their Anthology as you re-play the full audio version of the play on the **CD (file 2.1)**. Explain that the Power words are in bold in the Anthology text.
- Now ask the children to read their copy of the script with their partners, taking one adult and one child part each, and to read the words and phrases in bold with great expression! Explain that you will be listening in.
- Tell the children to choose three parts of the script to freeze-frame. Explain that a freeze-frame can be like a photograph – a snap shot of a particular moment in the play, e.g. they could freeze-frame the moment when Ria realises that Cameron has stolen her idea about the plate for Steve or the moment when Steve opens his presents.
- Remind them to think carefully about their body positions and facial expressions. Who will they be looking at? What are they feeling inside?
- Give them time to practise their freeze-frames and then select partnerships to 'hold' and show their frames to the class.
- Ask the rest of the children to discuss what part of the script they might be framing.
- Now tell the class to all hold their freeze-frames at the same time on a count of three.

noting ideas

Daily log

Purpose: for children to keep a personal reading, writing and thinking log to record thoughts and ideas for their own writing

- Ask the children to write two or three sentences in their Daily log about the funniest, most surprising, or disappointing present they have ever opened, explaining what their feelings were at the time.

effective discussion; provide justifications for their views

Big Question (CD)

Purpose: for children to develop their skills of argument and discussion through a mini enquiry session based on a philosophical question relating to the work of the day

- Display today's Big Question on the **CD (file 2.3)**:

  Is it easier to be a child or a grown-up?*

- Follow the process as explained at the end of Day 1 (p.139).

** This Big Question will be revisited on Day 11 – the first day of the Non-fiction week.*

DAY 3

Re-read a script version 3 A

Purpose: for children to deepen their understanding of the script by increasing familiarity with the text

Curriculum link: read silently, checking the script makes sense to them

- Ask the children to read the whole script silently from the Anthology pp.70–78. Tell them that they can stop to record any thoughts, ideas, questions, and favourite bits in their Daily log as they read the text. Explain that it is more important for them to think about what they are reading than to finish first and, as they know what happens, it doesn't matter if they don't finish this time.

Think and link 1 A CD

making comparisons, identifying themes

Purpose: for children to make links and connections with other stories and their own experiences

- Ask the children to look at the script in the Anthology pp.70–78 as you talk through each section, encouraging children to think about their own experiences and make links with other stories, films and plays they might know.
- TOL to model the thinking and linking. Use your own words and ideas or print off the 'script' below from **CD (file 3.1)** to help you:
  TOL: '*I used to fight with my older sister a lot because we shared a bedroom. We even tried to draw a chalk line on the floor to show my area and hers! My sister always used to run to Mum and get her side of the story out first. Do you have arguments with brothers and sisters, cousins, friends? Have you ever tried to get a grown-up on your side?*
  '*Lots of stories, films and plays are about families and rivalry between brothers and sisters. Remember in* Prometheus and Pandora *[in Unit 1] Epimetheus was jealous because his brother Prometheus could make models out of clay?*
  '*Oh and what about Cinderella? This is a fairy story that is often performed from a script, where two sisters treat their beautiful step-sister like a servant but she ends up marrying a prince! Have you ever seen it as a pantomime or a film?*'
- Ask children to TTYP to articulate and share ideas/connections. Collect feedback and paraphrase, clarify and extend their thoughts and ideas.

What's explicit, what's implicit? CD A PB

drawing inferences and justifying these with evidence

Purpose: for children to develop their ability to interpret text and sub-text

- Tell the children that the words on the page only give some of the story; to understand what characters might be thinking and what motivates them to act in particular ways we need to search for clues that might give us extra information.
- Explain that if the answer to the question draws on explicit information, you can find the answers in the text. If the question requires an answer that relies upon implicit information, you will have to work harder to answer because the answer is not written down.
- Display the grid showing examples of explicit text from the script **CD (file 3.2)**. Model how you find the first example in the Anthology p.70. TOL as you choose the most appropriate implicit text. Use drag and drop to place your selection in the grid.
- Now guide the children to find the next example of text in the Anthology and TTYP to choose the most appropriate example of implicit text. Remind the children that they will need to justify their answers.
- Collect feedback and use drag and drop to complete the grid.
- Now tell the children to look at the What's explicit, what's implicit? activity in the Pupils' Book p.57 to explore the text. Remind the children that there is no correct answer to some of the questions, just their own carefully considered opinions.

Curriculum link: noting and developing initial ideas

Daily log

Purpose: for children to keep a personal reading, writing and thinking log to record thoughts and ideas for their own writing

- Tell the children to write the email Ria was writing to her friend at the beginning of the play. In the email, Ria should briefly tell her friend what it is like having Cameron to stay. Ask the children to TTYP to share ideas first and then write in their Daily log.

effective discussion; provide justifications for their views

Big Question

Purpose: for children to develop their skills of argument and discussion through a mini enquiry session based on a philosophical question relating to the work of the day

- Display today's Big Question on the **CD (file 3.3):**

  What would life be like if we could see what other people were thinking?
- Follow the process as explained at the end of Day 1 (p.139).

DAY 4

drawing inferences and justifying with evidence, identifying key details that support ideas

What if not…?

Purpose: for children to consider how character, setting and plot affect each other

- Tell the children to look at the What if not…? questions in the Pupils' Book p.58. Model how you consider the first What if not…? What if not *humorous?* What if Steve were *grumpy?* Use TOL, to express your own ideas or print off the script from the **CD (file 4.1).**
- Ask children to TTYP and discuss this and the other What if not…? questions. Collect feedback and encourage others to build up the argument. Give your opinion too.

compare characters

Role on the wall

Purpose: for children to think more deeply about characters in the script and to record their ideas

- Before the lesson, print off a blank body outline for each set of partners from **CD (file 4.2)**.
- Display the body outline on the **CD (file 4.3)**. Explain that this Role on the wall represents the character of Lorraine. Drag and drop her name into the body.
- TOL as you select appropriate words and phrases to describe the character of Lorraine from the 'characteristics' options.
- Model using the text in the Anthology to verify or disprove your choices.
- Draw the children into your TOL, encouraging them to disagree by deliberately making a 'wrong' choice. Don't make it look too easy. Model being unsure, change your mind and ask the children to TTYP to help you to choose.
- Drag and drop the chosen words and phrases into the body shape.
- Give the children the blank body outlines and ask them to TTYP to complete at least one other role on the wall together for Steve, Ria or Cameron.
- Encourage the children to use their own words and phrases as well as the bank examples.
- Walk around as they talk and work, questioning choices, praising good partner work and good selections.
- Ask partners to cut out their outlines and stick them up on the board or on a wall. Pick out similarities and differences in choices to stimulate further discussion.

Curriculum link: discuss how authors use language

Formal/informal?

Purpose: for children to develop their understanding of the use of formal and informal language in scripts

- Tell the children that sometimes we change the way we speak because we are in different situations. We mostly speak *informally* at home with family and friends and *formally* in situations where we don't know someone very well or we are talking to someone in a formal setting, for example giving a talk in assembly.
- Display the grid on the **CD (file 4.4)**, click 'Reveal' to show examples of informal text and its equivalent formal version.
- Ask them to TTYP to use the Anthology to decide whether they think the dialogue in the *Father's Day* script is mostly formal or informal. Collect responses and clarify when necessary.

making comparisons

Daily log

Purpose: for children to keep a personal reading, writing and thinking log to record thoughts and ideas for their own writing

- Ask the children to draw a mind map showing their own family roles and characteristics. Suggest they have one branch to represent each person. Remind them to use symbols as well as words to show relationships and roles in the family.

effective discussion; provide justifications for their views

Big Question

Purpose: for children to develop their skills of argument and discussion through a mini enquiry session based on a philosophical question relating to the work of the day

- Display today's Big Question on the **CD (file 4.5)**:

  Are we different people in different situations?

- Follow the process explained at the end of Day 1 (p. 39).

DAY 5

asking questions to improve their understanding

The script store

Purpose: for children to be able to identify scripted and non-scripted material in broadcasts, and for children to develop their understanding of the link between audience and purpose in broadcasts

- Tell the children that scripts might be prepared and performed in front of an audience in order to: entertain (comedy film), give information (news report), persuade (advert), instruct someone how to do something (cookery programme), explain (documentary), argue or discuss (debate or discussion). Sometimes the purpose of a script will be a mixture of these, e.g. a play or film intended to entertain could also be persuasive; a news broadcast intended to give information could also be entertaining.
- Explain to the children what the term 'fly on the wall documentary' means.
- Tell the children that a real family, similar to the one in our playscript, was filmed for 12 weeks for a fly on the wall documentary about family life.
- Explain that they are now going see a video of a TV presenter who is about to do an interview with the family about the experience of being filmed all day long for the documentary and their family life. (N.B. The presenter only introduces the family, we don't see the whole interview.)
- Play the video on the **CD (file 5.1)**.
- Ask the children to TTYP to discuss whether the presenter is speaking informally or formally to the audience. Collect feedback and clarify as necessary.

- Explain that the presenter is going to interview the Greenidge children and ask them lots of questions and he will need them written down in a script.
- Ask the children to TTYP to think of at least three questions he could ask. The questions should be about what it was like having a film crew in the house, being recognised in the street, what their family is like, etc.
- Collect questions orally and model how to formalise the language to make it suitable for the TV presenter.
- Now ask the children to TTYP to discuss whether they think the family's replies to the questions will be scripted or unscripted. Encourage them to be prepared to support their answers.
- Collect feedback and clarify as necessary.

Dramatic improvisation PB

Purpose: for children to develop their empathetic responses to characters and develop their understanding of scripted and unscripted dialogue

- Tell the children that partner 1s will be the TV interviewer and partner 2s will be one of the children from the documentary family.
- Explain that partner 1s will ask questions A and B in the Dramatic improvisation activity in the Pupils' Book pp.58–59 and partner 2s will improvise answers in role.
- Tell them that they will swap roles and partner 2s will then ask questions C and D and partner 1s will improvise answers in role.
- Allow time to practise. Walk around noting and praising interesting questions and responses, and appropriate use of formal/informal language. Give oral feedback.

Curriculum link: asking questions to improve their understanding

Daily log

Purpose: for children to keep a personal reading, writing and thinking log to record thoughts and ideas for their own writing

- Ask the children to TTYP to discuss who they would most like to interview if they could be a TV presenter for a day. Tell them to record their answer in their Daily log and then write at least two questions they would ask.

effective discussion; provide justifications for their views

Big Question CD

Purpose: for children to develop their skills of argument and discussion through a mini enquiry session based on a philosophical question relating to the work of the day

- Display today's Big Question on the **CD (file 5.2)**:

  Is being famous the same as being important?

- Follow the process explained at the end of Day 1 (p.139).

WRITING FICTION

DAY 6

Build a character A CD

Purpose: for children to be able to use details to begin to build a character

describing characters

- Tell the children that you want to create a character for a script you are thinking of writing. Say that you have chosen to base your character around one of your favourite Power words from the *Father's Day* script: *malicious!*
- Point to the word on your Playscript wall and remind the children of where it was used in the *Father's Day* script in the Anthology p.71. Ask them to TTYP to

tell each other what the word means. Collect answers and repeat the definition and sentence from Day 2:

malicious – spiteful, unkind

That was a *malicious* trick to play on your friend!

- Explain that you are going to use the Role on the wall figure to record some words and phrases that will tell us more about this *malicious* character.
- Display the **CD (file 6.1)** to show the blank Role on the wall figure, the bank of words and phrases and the character statements.
- Read the statements and ask the children to help you to find one or more words or phrases that could match up with the statement. Drag and drop into the figure, for example:

  Statement: He scared the young children playing in the park.

  Word/phrase: *nasty, spiteful, a bully, frightening*
- Encourage the children to offer synonyms for the chosen words.

Curriculum link: describing characters

Show, don't tell

Purpose: for children to explore ways of developing characterisation by showing, rather than telling

- Explain that the character statements *tell us* what the character has done and the words inside the figure *tell us* what kind of person he is but you are now going to write a sentence that will *show us* what the character is like.
- Click on **CD (file 6.2)** to display the beginning of the process of developing one of the statements into a *telling* and then a *showing* sentence.
- Say the sentence: 'He went up to the young children playing in the park and told them to give him their football.' Then TOL about what the incident would really look like:

  'If I was an actor playing the part of this bully, what might I do with my face and body?'

  Mime the actions, stance, body language, facial expressions of the actions of a bully.

  'I've puffed up my chest and shoulders to make them look bigger.'

  'I've made my hands into clenched fists.'
- As the children do their own mini mime, ask them to freeze-frame. Walk round commenting, using appropriate and varied vocabulary to describe what you see.
- Open **CD (file 6.3)** and click 'TOL' to show the rest of the process of developing the *telling* sentence into a *showing* sentence.
- Now ask the children to look at the *telling* sentence in the Show don't tell activity in the Pupils' Book p.60 and TTYP to discuss how turn it into two or three *showing* sentences.
- When all the children have their opening sentence ready ask them to write.
- Collect feedback and scribe some good examples on the board.

learn the conventions of different types of writing

Build a speech

Purpose: for children to revise the conventions of writing speech in a script

- Remind the children that the malicious bully is going to be a character in a playscript.
- Display the Doing, feeling, thinking or saying grid on the **CD (file 6.4)**.
- TOL as you go through the two examples, drawing the children into the TOL and offering your own variations or additions.
- Now complete the rest of the grid as a whole class task, using TTYP and feedback, typing responses into the cells.

Curriculum link: making predictions, noting ideas

Daily log

Purpose: for children to keep a personal reading, writing and thinking log to record thoughts and ideas for their own writing

- Ask the children to TTYP to predict a situation in a script in which the character might appear. Tell them to record one of the ideas in note form in their Daily log.

effective discussion; provide justifications for their views

Big Question

Purpose: for children to develop their skills of argument and discussion through a mini enquiry session based on a philosophical question relating to the work of the day

- Display today's Big Question on the **CD (File 6.5)**:

  What makes us who we are?

- Follow the process as explained at the end of Day 1 (p.139).

DAY 7

plan writing by noting and developing ideas; consider how authors have developed characters and settings

Build a script 1 (CD)

Purpose: for children to be able to see a script grow through three stages of development

- Remind the children that they heard two versions of *Father's Day* (Script versions 1 and 2) before they heard and read the full script. It *prepared* them to read the full script.
- Explain that you are going to show them two versions of a new script to be written. These versions *prepared* the writer to write the full script. Show Build a script 1 statements on the **CD (file 7.1)** and explain that these were the prompts that helped the writer to know what to put in the new script.
- Now display Build a script 1 on the **CD (file 7.2)**. Read aloud to the children. Explain that you are now going to show them another version of the new script to be written. This one has additional information and words – it has been developed.

Build a script 2 (CD)

Purpose: for children to be able to see a story grow through three stages of development

- Show Build a script 2 on the **CD (file 7.3)**. TOL as you compare this version with Build a script 1. Click 'Highlights' to show additional information, names and adjectives. Point out the synonyms *cross/annoyed* and *rescued/retrieved* to the children.

using similar writing as models for their own

Build a script 3 (CD)

Purpose: for children to see an example of writing that will provide a model for their own writing

- An example script is provided as a model for writing. You are in role as the writer of this script during these activities.
- Display the script on the **CD (file 7.4)**. Explain that when writing this script your purpose was to entertain and interest the audience or reader and also to make them think about relationships with family and friends.
- Read 'your' script (Build a script 3) to the children.

noting ideas, provide reasoned justifications for their views

Daily log

Purpose: for children to keep a personal reading, writing and thinking log to record thoughts and ideas for their own writing

- Ask the children to share ideas for a title for the script. Ask them to record their best idea in their Daily log and explain why they think it is a good title.

Curriculum link: effective discussion; provide justifications for their views

Big Question

Purpose: for children to develop their skills of argument and discussion through a mini enquiry session based on a philosophical question relating to the work of the day

- Display today's Big Question on the **CD (File 7.5)**:

  Should bullies be punished or helped?
- Follow the process as explained at the end of Day 1 (p.139).

DAY 8

assessing the effectiveness of others' writing

Evaluation

Purpose: for children to develop their ability to evaluate the effectiveness of a piece of writing

- Ask the children to TTYP to read the script together, printed from the **CD (file 8.1)**, taking two parts each – whichever partner reads Katy's part should also read the stage directions.
- Using TTYP and oral feedback, ask the children to evaluate the writing using the Evaluation guide questions in the Pupils' Book p.60. Collect feedback and encourage discussion and constructive argument.

understand, through being shown, the skills and processes essential for writing

Write a script 1

Purpose: for children to develop their confidence and skills in script planning and development

- Explain that you want to add a scene to the end of the script.
- Show the bare bones of the extra scene on the **CD (file 8.2)** Write a script 1. Read it aloud.

Write a script 2

Purpose: for children to develop their confidence and skills in script planning and development

- Keep **CD (file 8.2)** on display.
- Using TOL, and encouraging the children to offer their ideas, model how to develop speech 1 by adding or changing words and phrases. TOL about stage directions and model the conventions of writing them in a script. Write on a flipchart or large sheet of paper, for example:

  PCSO: What happened then lads?

  TOL: '*What would he do when he is interviewing the children? Would he take his hat off if he's indoors? Yes, I think so… I'll need stage directions there then. I expect they might look a bit nervous so the officer will try to sound friendly but it is a serious conversation so he will be quite formal. He has to get all the information he needs so I'll make him sound kind and encouraging…*

  PCSO: *(Taking his hat off)* Right then lads, why don't you tell me exactly what happened? *(Gets out a black notebook and pen)* Ben, you go first but take your time.
- Repeat using speech 2.

  Ben: This big lad tried to steal our ball.
- Now ask the children to help you to develop speech 3 using TTYP to allow discussion and ideas for the character's lines and appropriate stage directions. Emphasise that they should use the text in the example as a starting point to build upon.
- Tell the children to develop speeches and stage directions for numbers 4 and 5 using the Write a script 2 prompts in the Pupils' Book p.61. Tell them to compose their speech individually in their heads first. They must make sure they can say their opening speech to their partner before they start to write.

Curriculum link: considering how authors have developed characters

Daily log

Purpose: for children to keep a personal reading, writing and thinking log to record thoughts and ideas for their own writing

- Ask the children TTYP and discuss which character they think is the weakest in the script. Tell them to think carefully about the different ways people can be weak or strong. Then ask them to write their ideas down in their Daily log.

effective discussion; provide justifications for their views

Big Question (CD)

Purpose: for children to develop their skills of argument and discussion through a mini enquiry session based on a philosophical question relating to the work of the day

- Display today's Big Question on the **CD (file 8.3)**:

  Is it always wrong to take something that isn't yours?

- Follow the process as explained at the end of Day 1 (p.139).

DAY 9

writing

Write a script 3 (PB)

Purpose: for children to use the speeches and stage directions they have already developed to write a whole extra scene

- Tell the children that they are now ready to write their own, extended version of the extra scene – Scene 4. Ask them to use the Write a script 2 composition prompts in the Pupils' Book p.61. Remind them to use any useful parts of their Daily log to help them and to look at the Playscript wall for words and phrases, and a thesaurus for synonyms.
- Encourage children to rehearse their opening sentence with their partners before they begin to write.
- Remind them of the speeches you modelled but encourage them to use their own ideas, add more speeches between characters and think of a suitable ending to the scene.

DAY 10

assessing the effectiveness of their own and others' writing

Share a script

Purpose: for children to be able to look critically at their writing

- Ask the children to read through their own scripts, underlining their favourite or best parts. Ask them to share these with their partners. Collect feedback on best bits from partners.
- Make sure that any powerful or rarer words or phrases used are added to the Playscript wall.

Evaluate and edit (CD)

Purpose: for children to evaluate their own and their partner's work against specific criteria and then discuss how they could improve their work

- Display **CD (file 10.1)** to show the evaluation prompts and read them together using MT/YT.
- As a model, select an example of work from the children where the writing has met the criteria, and share this with the other children, explaining why it works well.
- Tell the children to take turns to read their partner's writing and discuss how well they have met the criteria.
- Ask children to discuss at least two changes they could make to improve their work following the partner discussion.

Curriculum link: proofread for spelling and punctuation errors

Proofread

Purpose: for children to proofread their work and make changes to improve the accuracy of their grammar, punctuation and spelling

- Now ask the children to proofread their work. If you have noticed that several children need to improve on a particular aspect of spelling, grammar or punctuation, use this as a focus for the Proofread activity. Write an example which includes common errors from the children's writing and use this as a model
- The children should always be checking for standard use of punctuation and correct spelling of common exception words.
- The following points would be relevant as the particular focus for this Unit:
  - using playscript conventions correctly, e.g. *names before dialogue, stage directions* and *scene descriptions*
  - checking commas have been used correctly
  - checking any contractions are spelled correctly and used in informal speech
  - checking for correct use of punctuation, particularly exclamation marks to show a command, question marks and ellipses.

effective discussion; provide justifications for their views, distinguish between fact and opinion

Very Big Question

Purpose: for children to develop a willingness to broaden or revise their opinions through exploring one of the Big Questions in more depth

- See Unit 1 Day 10 for teaching notes on the Very Big Question (p.36).

Discussion texts

READING AND WRITING NON-FICTION

The non-fiction part of the Unit links to the fiction by exploring script forms such as broadcast scripts on non-fiction themes. Discussion texts are studied, looking at the conventions of oral debate. Children write a scripted speech and use it to debate whether junk food should be banned or not. They also write a discussion text.

See p.134 for the daily timetable for the Non-fiction week.

Non-fiction

Reading

Children will:

- learn about the terms *balanced, bias, personal* and *impersonal* and how to recognise them in issue-based texts
- identify the conventions of oral and written debates
- learn about the purpose of a transcript
- discuss the effectiveness of a transcript for a live studio debate.

Writing

Key writing purpose to be shared with the children:

To write a balanced text about whether or not junk food should be banned.

Writing evaluation to be shared with the children

My discussion text:

- is balanced (looks at both sides of the argument)
- summarises the debate in a final paragraph.

Grammar:

- includes adverbs and adverbials that help to contrast the two ideas or arguments, e.g. *on the other hand, however, other people believe*
- is written in a formal, impersonal style to show my reader it is a balanced text, not my own opinions.

See the Planning section of the Software ('Timetables' tab) for a printable version of the Writing purpose and evaluation.

DAY 11

Curriculum link: learn the conventions of different types of writing

Introduction (CD)

Purpose: for children to revise their existing knowledge of discussion texts using the context of one of the Big Questions and the scripts studied in weeks 1 and 2.

- Explain that we used all of our Big Questions as the basis for discussion. We have discussed the Big Questions and listened to different points of view that were given in spoken word form – orally.
- Show the Big Question from Day 2, *Is it easier to be a child or a grown-up?* on the **CD (file 2.3)**.
- Ask the children to TTYP to recall some of the points they discussed. Collect feedback.
- Explain that because we each had an opportunity to put forward our point of view and listen to others', we had a balanced discussion: some people thought it was easier to be a grown-up, *on the other hand*, some people thought it was easier to be a child.
- Say that if we care very deeply about something, we might try to persuade others to agree with us. If two people disagree, they might discuss and argue, and to help to persuade each other, they might use examples to convince others that they are right.
- Remind the children that in the play *Father's Day*, the characters' speeches were not balanced, they were biased – each character gave us information from their own, personal point of view, especially when they talked directly to the audience.

exploring the meaning of words in context

Word power (CD) (PB)

Purpose: for children to become familiar with some words and synonyms associated with discussion texts

discuss persuade balanced biased personal impersonal

- Before the lesson, print the words and their definitions from the **CD (file 11.1)** and display on your Non-fiction wall.
- Look at the words and their definitions with the children explaining that they are all words we use when we talk about discussion texts.
- Now read the sentences to the children from the Pupils' Book p.62. Ask the children to repeat the sentences using MT/YT.
- The children must hear you use the word in your teaching and conversation throughout the day, for example:
  'Well done, you gave a *balanced* report of the incident on the playground.'
  'I think our classroom is the best, but I am *biased*!'
  'You can make your Daily log more *personal* by decorating it.'
  'You were not directly involved so you can tell me what happened in a more *impersonal* way.'
- Now tell the children to do the Word power activity in the Pupils' Book p.62.

distinguish between statements of fact and opinion

Balance and bias (CD) (PB)

Purpose: for children to be able to recognise bias and balance in issue-based texts

- Display the extracts from different issue-based texts on the **CD (file 11.2)**.
- Read each text out loud to the children (explain what a blog is if necessary).
- Ask the children to look at the texts in the Balance and bias activity in the Pupils' Book pp.62–63 and TTYP to identify the central issue or topic in each text.
- Collect feedback and use TOL as you clarify as necessary.

- Remind the children of the words 'balance' and 'bias' and their definitions. Point to them on your Non-fiction wall.
- Display the grid, **CD (file 11.3)** and TOL as you identify Text A as a biased text. Don't make it look too easy, hesitate and draw the children into your thought process.
- Print copies of the grid **CD (file 11.4)** for each set of partners or one each.
- Ask them to TTYP to identify balance and bias in the rest of the texts. Remind them that sometimes it is not clear cut, in which case ask them to decide what it is most likely to be. Tell the children to complete the grid once they have decided.
- Collect feedback and clarify as necessary.

Curriculum link: learn the conventions of different types of writing

Personal and impersonal CD PB

Purpose: for children to be able to recognise personal and impersonal language in issue-based texts

- Display the first extract again on the **CD (file 11.5)**. TOL as you spot clues that help you to identify the style of the language used – is it personal or impersonal?
- Show the grid with the personal box ticked on the **CD (file 11.6)**.
- Now ask the children to look at the texts again in the Pupils' Book p.63 and TTYP to discuss which use personal language and which use impersonal language.
- Tell them to tick the box in the grid when they agree.

Daily log

Purpose: for children to keep a personal reading, writing and thinking log to record thoughts and ideas for their own writing

- Tell the children to re-read text B about dogs in parks in the Pupils' Book p.63. Ask them write a short email or letter to the newspaper from a dog lover who is outraged by the suggestion that they should be banned from parks. Encourage them to use the same personal, emotive style as text B.

DAY 12

reading non-fiction

Deconstruction 1 A

Purpose: for children to be able to identify the conventions of oral debate

- Ask the children to find the studio debate text in the Anthology pp.79–80.
- Explain what a transcript is (a written copy of what people say, for example in a speech, debate or interview) and say that this text is a transcript of a live studio debate. Point to the word 'debate' on your Non-fiction wall as you speak.
- Read the transcript out loud to the children using lots of enthusiasm, expression and intonation. Collect feedback.

Year 5 Grammar using commas to clarify meaning or avoid ambiguity

Grammar: commas CD PB HB

Purpose: for children to understand how commas can be used to clarify meaning and avoid ambiguity in text

- Write the word 'comma' on the board and ask the children to TTYP and talk about what commas are used for. Take feedback, drawing out that we use commas to mark a pause, in order to separate parts of a sentence. This can include separating items in a list.
- Display the **CD (file 12.1)**. Explain that this a description of a birthday tea, but the writer has missed out all the commas. Remind the children of the punctuation mime for a comma (see CD Planning/Extras). Read out the description but ask the children to do the punctuation mime for a comma when they hear a pause where

a comma should be. Then click 'Highlight' to reveal the corrected text, with the commas highlighted.

- Explain that commas are important because they can change what a sentence means. Click to the next slide to display two versions of a speech bubble from the Big Debate text in the Anthology. Point out that in the first speech bubble, there are two commas in the first sentence, but in the second speech bubble, there is just one.
- Use MT/YT to read out each sentence and ask the children to TTYP to talk about the difference in meaning between the two. Take feedback, drawing out that in the first speech bubble, 'you know' is just a casual comment after the comma, but in the second speech bubble, the lack of comma could mean that he is a doctor that the children actually know! Explain that when there is more than one meaning, we call it 'ambiguity'. Write the word on the board and ask the children to say it several times.
- Click to the next slide and read out the sentence, taking care not to insert any pauses. Then ask the children to describe the funny picture this makes in their minds. If necessary, read the sentence again. Click 'Reveal' to show the picture of the seagulls eating ice-cream and playing cricket on the beach.
- Ask the children to TTYP to discuss where they would add the comma to avoid ambiguity and to make more sense of the sentence. Take feedback, confirming that the comma should be inserted after the word 'seagulls', to make it part of a list of activities, rather than just a description of what the seagulls did.
- Ask the children to look at the Grammar: commas activity on p.64 of their Pupils' Book. Tell them to TTYP to complete the activity orally, then take feedback with the whole class.

Homework Book p.23 provides further practice on commas.

Curriculum link: explain and discuss their understanding of what they have read including through debates

Role-play 1

Purpose: for children to be able to practise using clear language to express a point of view

- Tell the children that all the partner 1s are going to argue *for* junk food being banned and all the partners 2s are going to argue *against* junk food being banned.
- Tell partner 1s to get into groups of four to think of arguments *for* banning junk food. Tell all the partner 2s to do the same to think of arguments *against*.
- When they have done this they should rejoin their usual partners.
- Now ask the children to role-play the debate, with Partner 1s and Partner 2s taking turns to speak.
- Walk round listening in and noting use of appropriate language, persuasive arguments, following the 'rules' of debate (not interrupting, listening to each other, etc.) to mention in your feedback.

retrieve, record and present information from non-fiction

Daily log

Purpose: for children to keep a personal reading, writing and thinking log to record thoughts and ideas for their own writing

- Ask the children to TTYP to come up with at least two issues that people have different views about. Collect feedback and make a generic list. If possible, use the Internet to look at children's news and current affairs websites (children's TV news programmes have good websites). Look at which issues are currently being presented and discussed on the chat or forum pages. Tell the children to make a note of which issues they are most interested in and have strong views about in their Daily log.

DAY 13

Curriculum link: record and present information from non-fiction

Write a discussion 1 (CD)

Purpose: for children to develop their understanding of the conventions of oral debate

- Explain that the whole class is going to role-play a live studio debate. (You will need to play the role of the host and man/woman with the microphone.)
- Tell the children they are going to adopt two roles in the debate. One is a member of the studio audience who is for the banning of junk food and the other is someone who is against.
- Use the **CD (file 13.1)** to display the list of roles/characters to choose from. It doesn't matter if they duplicate roles as their arguments may still be different.
- Ask the children to write a short scripted speech for each of their roles, for and against banning junk food, making just one persuasive point in each speech.
- When they are ready, ask them to TTYP to check each other's scripts make sense and are not too long.

explain and discuss their understanding through debates

Role-play 2

Purpose: for children to develop their public speaking skills

- Conduct a 'studio' debate making it as realistic as possible. The children can choose which one of their two roles to take and if time allows, they can switch roles to give their second speech.
- Make sure you sum up at the end and have a proper vote!

provide reasoned justifications for their views

Daily log

Purpose: for children to keep a personal reading, writing and thinking log to record thoughts and ideas for their own writing

- Ask the children to TTYP to discuss two things they thought worked well in the debate, e.g. having a chairperson, taking turns, taking for and against roles, and two things that could have been better and record them in their Daily log.

DAY 14

using similar writing as models for their own

Deconstruction 2 (CD)

Purpose: for children to see an example of writing that will provide a model for their own writing

- Explain that if we have a discussion about a topic in written form only, we need to organise the text to show:
  - a balanced statement of the issue
  - phrases that help to contrast two ideas or arguments
  - arguments supporting one side of the issue
  - evidence or examples to make each argument more powerful or convincing
  - arguments supporting the other side of the issue.
- Display **CD (file 14.1)** to show the Animals in captivity extract. Read it out loud to the children.
- Click 'Highlights' to show the key features of the discussion text.
- Tell the children that you want to write a discussion text based on the junk food debate.
- Explain that you are going to use a grid to help you to organise your ideas and to focus on the features of a discussion text.
- Display the grid on **CD (file 14.2)** showing the deconstructed text. TOL as you show how to use the grid to organise your ideas.

Curriculum link: plan their writing, noting and developing initial ideas

Write a discussion 2

Purpose: for children to be able to use a variety of resources to make a plan for a piece of writing

- Give each child a printed copy of **CD (file 14.3)**.
- Tell the children they are going to complete the grid to provide a plan to help them to write their own discussion text on whether junk food should be banned.
- To help them to think of good arguments for and against, remind them to use the junk food debate transcript in the Anthology pp.79–80, their own studio debate speeches and experience and any relevant notes in their Daily log.

provide reasoned justifications for their views

Daily log

Purpose: for children to keep a personal reading, writing and thinking log to record thoughts and ideas for their own writing

- Ask the children to decide which are the most powerful arguments for and against banning junk food and record them in their Daily log.

DAY 15

writing non-fiction

Write a discussion 3

Purpose: for children to develop their ability to use appropriate language, form and content to present an issue in a discussion text

- Tell the children that they are going to write their own discussion text.
- Remind them to:
  - use their completed planning grids to organise their text
  - start a new paragraph for each new argument
  - rehearse their first sentence with their partners before writing
  - read each sentence as soon as they have written in down, to check it makes sense.
- Ask the children to use the Write a discussion text 3 prompts in the Pupils' Book p.64 as a guide.
- Explain to the children that once they have written their discussion texts, you will look at how to sum up the main arguments. They do not need to include a summary in their texts at this point.

summarising the main ideas

Summarise

Purpose: for children to develop their ability to summarise arguments

- Tell the children that the writer of a discussion text needs a short, final paragraph to sum up the main arguments.
- Explain that the writer could also show which viewpoint they support now that the arguments have been given.
- Say that it is also a final opportunity for the reader to weigh up the fors and againsts and make up their own mind.
- Display the **CD (file 15.1)** to show examples of two short, concluding paragraphs and use TTYP to answer the questions shown on the CD.
- Now show the **CD (file 15.2)** to model how to write a conclusion. TOL as you show the completed parts of the grid and then use TTYP and feedback to complete the empty cells.
- Type the children's ideas into the cells.
- Now ask the children to write two or three sentences to sum up the main arguments in their discussion texts. Remind them to rehearse their first sentence with their partner before writing it down.
- Use an ICT slot for children to type up their discussion texts as a piece of continuous prose, using their completed grids.

Curriculum link: assessing the effectiveness of their own and others' writing

Evaluate and edit (CD)

Purpose: *for children to evaluate their own and their partner's work against specific criteria and then discuss how they could improve their work*

- Display **CD (file 15.3)** to show the evaluation prompts and read them together using MT/YT.
- As a model, select an example of work from the children where the writing has met the criteria, and share this with the other children, explaining why it works well.
- Tell the children to take turns to read their partner's writing and discuss how well they have met the criteria.
- Ask children to discuss at least two changes they could make to improve their work following the partner discussion.

proofread for spelling and punctuation errors

Proofread

Purpose: *for children to proofread their work and make changes to improve the accuracy of their grammar, punctuation and spelling*

- Now ask the children to proofread their work. If you have noticed that several children need to improve on a particular aspect of spelling, grammar or punctuation, use this as a focus for the Proofread activity. Write an example which includes common errors from the children's writing and use this as a model.
- The children should be checking for standard use of punctuation and correct spelling of common exception words.
- The following points would be relevant as the particular focus for this Unit:
  - checking for correct use of commas to make the meaning clear
  - checking that paragraphs have been used correctly
  - checking for correct use of question marks and exclamation marks.

Curriculum coverage chart

England	*Literacy and Language* Year 5 is closely matched to the Programmes of study for the new *National Curriculum in England* from 2014 and the Year 5 grammar requirements listed in its Grammar appendix. See the overview chart on p.18 and the curriculum link boxes in the teaching notes for details. *Literacy and Language* is suitable for children working at National Curriculum level 2a and above and aims to take children to level 5 and beyond. See **www.oxfordprimary.co.uk** for curriculum updates.
Scotland	Primary 6 *Curriculum for Excellence* Second level
Wales	*Literacy and Language* enables children to become accomplished in • oracy across the curriculum • reading across the curriculum • writing across the curriculum. See **www.oxfordprimary.co.uk** for further details and a free downloadable correlation chart when the new *National Literacy and Numeracy Framework* is introduced.
Northern Ireland	Primary 6/Year 6 The following points from the *Language and Literacy* curriculum are covered in each unit of *Literacy and Language*: *Unit 1* Talking and listening: 1, 2, 3, 5, 6, 7, 8, 9, 10, 13, Reading: 1, 3, 4, 5, 6, 7, 8, 9, 10, 11, 13 Writing: 1, 2, 4, 5, 6, 7, 8, 9, 10, 12 *Unit 2* Talking and listening: 1, 2, 3, 5, 7, 8, 9, 10, 13, Reading: 1, 3, 4, 5, 6, 7, 8, 9, 10, 11, 13 Writing: 1, 2, 4, 5, 6, 7, 8, 9, 10, 12 *Unit 3* Talking and listening: 1, 2, 3, 5, 7, 8, 9, 10, 12, 13 Reading: 1, 3, 4, 5, 6, 7, 8, 9, 10, 11, 13 Writing: 1, 2, 3, 4, 5, 6, 7, 8, 9, 10, 12 *Unit 4* Talking and listening: 1, 2, 3, 5, 7, 8, 9, 10, 12, 13 Reading: 1, 3, 4, 5, 6, 7, 8, 9, 10, 11, 13 Writing: 1, 2, 4, 5, 6, 7, 8, 9, 10, 12 *Unit 5* Talking and listening: 1, 2, 3, 5, 7, 8, 9, 10, 13 Reading: 1, 3, 4, 5, 6, 7, 8, 9, 10, 11, 13 Writing: 1, 2, 4, 5, 6, 7, 8, 9, 10, 12 *Unit 6* Talking and listening: 1, 2, 3, 5, 7, 8, 9, 10, 13 Reading: 1, 3, 4, 5, 6, 7, 8, 9, 10, 11, 13 Writing: 1, 2, 4, 5, 6, 7, 8, 9, 10, 12